Cranberries & Canada Geese

Webber's Northern Lodges

A Second Batch of
Our Most Requested Recipes

By
Helen Webber
&
Marie Woolsey

Cranberries & Canada Geese

by
Helen Webber & Marie Woolsey

Second Printing — January 2000

Published by
Blueberries & Polar Bears Publishing
P.O. Box 304
Churchill, Manitoba
Canada   R0B 0E0

Canadian Cataloguing in Publication Data

Webber, Helen, 1947 -

   Cranberries & Canada geese

   Includes index.
   ISBN 1-895292-62-X

1. Cookery.   I. Woolsey, Marie, 1942 -
II.   Title.

TX751.W433   1996   641.5   C96-920032-3

Cover Painting and Illustrations by:
Barbara Stone
Longmont, Colorado, U.S.A.

Photography on site at North Knife Lake by:
Ross (Hutch) Hutchinson, Hutchinson and Company
Calgary, Alberta

Inuit Carvings Compliments of:
Arctic Co-operatives Ltd.
Transportation of Inuit Carvings Compliments of *CalmAir*
Canadi⟩n *Partner*

Denby Dishes Compliments of:
David Shaw Tableware, Downsview, Ontario

Designed, Printed and Produced in Canada by:
Centax Books, a Division of PrintWest Communications Ltd.
Publishing Director, Photo Designer & Food Stylist: Margo Embury
1150 Eighth Avenue, Regina, Saskatchewan, Canada S4R 1C9
      (306) 525-2304   FAX: (306) 757-2439

Table of Contents

Recipes have been tested in U.S. Standard measurements. Common metric measurements are given as a convenience for those who are more familiar with metric. Recipes have not been tested in metric.

Dymond Lake Seasoning (DLS) is used in many of our recipes. It is our own unique blend of herbs and spices. It contains no MSG. If you are unable to find DLS, seasoned salt and/or seasoned pepper may be substituted. For each recipe that uses DLS, we have suggested appropriate alternatives. These vary from recipe to recipe to try to approximate the special flavors that DLS emphasizes in each recipe. To order Dymond Lake Seasoning, see page 207.

Introduction

Writing a book is a little like starting out on a canoe trip for the first time – you choose waters that have been well charted, but you are still surprised at what awaits you around each bend. If the experience is challenging, exciting and exhilarating, you can hardly wait to go again. *Cranberries & Canada Geese* is our second trip!

Since the release of *Blueberries & Polar Bears*, two years ago, we have become more aware of the popularity of wild meat all across Canada. It is offered in the best restaurants in Montreal, Toronto, Calgary and Vancouver and sold in more and more butcher shops. We have also met many people who have wild game in their freezers and don't know what to do with it! In *Cranberries & Canada Geese*, we have tried to respond to this trend – it is certainly nothing new – most of these recipes have been around for a long time, and have only needed to be revived. So, once again, we bring you Moose Goose & Things That Swim – more wonderful ways to prepare wild game and fish. In addition, Doug gives some instructions on the hanging and aging of wild game as well as cold-smoking for fish.

But *Cranberries & Canada Geese* also responds to the many cooks who thanked us in person, by phone or mail for making our recipes easy to follow, with ingredients they already had on hand. They asked for more of the same, and here it is! – more tested and true recipes from the Lodges, our families and friends.

And finally, we had a very positive response to our stories, jokes and graces and have tried to fit in as many new ones as possible. We also hope you will enjoy the Goose Facts – things you may not have known about Canada Geese – the bird that gives Canada its name!

What Were Canada Geese Called Before Confederation?

Well, one thing's for sure – they weren't called British North American geese. Their name, Canada geese, was bestowed on them long before the founding of the country; although both names share the same origins.

In 1758, the geese were given their English name, based on what the Indians called the birds. "Kanata" is a Huron word that means "village" or "settlement". The Hurons named the geese Kanata because the birds bred near Indian settlements.

Kanata was also the name the Indians gave to the French settlement of Stadacona, now known as Quebec city. In both cases, "Kanata" was corrupted to "Canada." Given the sequence of events, it looks like the country was named after the birds rather than visa versa.

From Good Question Book vol. 3 "What the Heck is a Grape Nut?" published by Script Publishing Inc. (Script: the writers' group). Copyright 1991 by Script and the Canadian Broadcasting Corporation.

 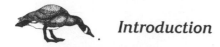 *Introduction*

From Helen & Marie

When Marie and Gary moved to Calgary, Gary's job changed from being a Bishop "on the road" to being the rector of a parish, and, basically, at home. Then Marie started travelling. She claims it is her turn! Helen has travelled with Doug to promote the Lodges for many years. With the book, she has had even more time away from home. As co-authors we have travelled throughout Canada promoting our book. We have gone places and done things that we never imagined in our wildest dreams, a cooking demo on television – a computer course for bookkeeping and accounting! Has it been exciting? You bet! We are indebted to the many friends and retailers who hosted book launchings. (We'd like to thank the lady who recognized us in a dress shop in Kenora, Ontario, and made us feel famous!) We are grateful to Ellen Lee who helps Marie with public appearances in Calgary, and never objects to being mistaken for a "famous author".

During the photo session for *Blueberries & Polar Bears*, we "kiddingly" said to Hutch and Linda (the photographers) and Margo (the Publishing Director), "if we do another book, we should do the pictures on location." So, North Knife it was! They arrived in August with all kinds of equipment and props. It had rained for most of the month, so we were very concerned – we were counting on sunshine for outdoor shots! Well, we were truly blessed (Could it be Marie's husband's influence?). The sun came out and stayed out for the next 3 days – in fact, within minutes of the completion of the last picture, the rain, once again, covered the earth!

The pictures were well worth the extra effort. Margo, Linda and Hutch went off with Doug to scout a suitable site (How could they choose amidst such beauty?). We were busy in the kitchen cooking the edible props. At the given time, we packed the food and headed for the site by boat, ATV or on foot. Two shots were taken at Helen's Falls – which can only be reached when the water is high, and this August it was as high as we've ever seen it – the river rose 9 feet overnight! But the rain that hid blueberries, beaches and picnic tables underwater brought a bumper mushroom crop which Margo used to good advantage in the pictures. The arrival of unexpected guests during the picture shoot only increased the challenge (and didn't hurt our image as supercooks, either!). It was an intense 3 days, but a time we thoroughly enjoyed and will never forget.

As with all projects of this type, we had lots of help. A big thank you to Heidi, Jim and Jason Shultz from Santa Barbara. Jim helped scout locations (and took Hutch fishing after work); Jason contributed a fresh lake trout for our hors d'oeuvres shot; and Heidi tackled mounds of dishes! The Arctic Co-operative Ltd. kindly supplied Inuit Carvings for the pictures. Their beauty enhanced the natural surroundings and added a "Northern Touch". Calm Air Ltd. provided transportation for the carvings. And a final thank you to our husbands and families whose support is so crucial and to whom we are eternally grateful.

CCCofffee PPIleeease! (Bear vs. Helicopter)

It was a regular morning at Dymond Lake. All the hunters were in the field, and we were busy in the kitchen with lunch and dinner preparations, when we heard a helicopter coming – not unusual, as Resources come in by helicopter a couple of times a season to check on things and they stop for coffee and a chat. I immediately put on some fresh coffee and started to get out some cookies, while Doug headed out to where the helicopter was landing. A couple of minutes later he came in with a fellow who looked half frozen and pretty shook up. All he told us was that a polar bear had beaten up on his helicopter at Seal River and he had flown in with no wind screen. We got him warmed up and fed, and sent him on his way to Churchill to get his helicopter fixed.

Later that day, my brother, Bruce, landed with his son, Fred, and nephew, Martin, on board. They had also just come from Seal River and Bruce proceeded to tell us the story of the wounded helicopter. He had flown up to Seal River to do some goose hunting with the boys. There was another small plane there already, which belonged to a couple of American fellows who were staying in the same abandoned cabin. They all went to bed fairly early, but were wakened sometime during the night by a bear trying to get into the cabin. They succeeded in scaring it off and went back to bed for awhile. Just before daybreak, Bruce and the boys headed out to go goose hunting. As they got near the runway, they could see the bear and this time it was pounding away on Bruce's airplane. Bruce knew he had to get rid of the bear before it destroyed the plane but he was not too keen on shooting it. He tried yelling and waving his arms to scare it off but the bear wasn't going anywhere. In fact it came around the plane towards them. So, with the 13- and 14-year-old boys there to back him up, if necessary, he fired a shot at the bear. To his alarm, his shotgun fell apart in his hands! He turned around to grab a gun from one of the boys, but they had run off and were hiding behind a rock! Luckily, for all of them, the bear took off into the bush and Bruce was able to get to his plane where he had another shotgun. But now he had a wounded bear on the loose and, as he looked around, he spotted a helicopter that had not been there the night before. It was a mess! The windscreen was smashed to bits, the seats had been torn out and were lying on the ground, there were bits and pieces of personal gear all over the place, and no sign of a pilot. He and the boys were looking around apprehensively, when the door of the plane belonging to the Americans opened very cautiously, and out climbed the pilot of the helicopter, looking very shaken. It turned out that he had landed near dark the night before, on his way to Churchill, and he did not know where the cabin was. So, rather than stumbling around in the dark he decided to catch a few winks in the helicopter until daylight. But, finding it quite uncomfortable, he moved to the airplane where he would be able to stretch out a bit better. Shortly after climbing in and dozing off, something woke him up. When he peered out the window, he could dimly see the bear demolishing his helicopter and there wasn't a thing he could do about it! The bear then came and gave the airplane he was in a few bats and pushes with his paws, but then it wandered off and stayed away until it came back to work on Bruce's plane. Needless to say, the poor man had lain there, in a state of shock and fright, until Bruce and the boys showed up. They helped him patch up his machine as best they could and that is when Bruce told him to stop and warm up with us at Dymond Lake! We never saw him again, but I'm willing to bet that he hasn't spent another night in a plane in polar bear country!

Moose, Goose
&
Things That Swim

We had no idea when we did "Blueberries & Polar Bears" that this section would be so well received. In fact, with antihunting lobbies so strong in some areas, we were a little apprehensive about it, but, as we suspected, there are many people out there who are just as enthusiastic as we are about experimenting with wild game. In fact, there is a growing interest across the continent in cooking with wild game. The most fashionable restaurants in Europe and Asia have long prized wild meats and now these unique flavors are becoming more available with game farms and culling of wild herds providing top-quality meat. We have done more experimenting and more sleuthing (Helen's brother-in-law, Gavin, is quite used to having us pull out a pen and paper after he has once again served a delicious "wild" dish) to bring you yet another collection of great recipes for Moose, Goose & Things That Swim!

Venison Hot Shots

Zesty and flavorful in a thin, crisp batter, these appetizers are a sure hit.

> **whole, pickled, jalapeño peppers**
> **cream cheese**
> **venison cutlets, cut in strips**
> **Predator Batter (below)**

1. Split jalapeños; remove the seeds. Fill each jalapeño with cream cheese. Roll the cutlet around the jalapeño; secure with a toothpick. Dip in batter and deep-fry, until venison is cooked, about 3 minutes.
2. You may also just stuff the pepper with creamed cheese, dip it in the batter and deep-fry.

See photograph on page 121.

Predator Batter

Brought to Dymond Lake by a hunter, this crisp batter is also great with fish.

1 cup	flour	250 mL
1	egg	1
1 tbsp.	baking powder	15 mL
1 tbsp.	baking soda	15 mL
12 oz.	beer	340 mL

1. Whisk together all ingredients and let sit for 30 minutes before using.

Barbecued Caribou Steak

When we arrived in Churchill from Dymond Lake this fall, we found that Paul, one of our trusty goose guides, had decided we should have dinner cooked for us for a change. Well, he didn't get any argument from Marie, Sandy or me. After all, we had been cooking for about 25 people from four in the morning until nine at night for the last three weeks. This is what he had whipped up for us!

	caribou steaks, OR deer, moose OR elk	
	DLS* OR seasoned salt and pepper	
½ cup	soy sauce	125 mL
½ cup	vinegar	125 mL
½ cup	red OR white wine	125 mL
½ cup	sugar	125 mL
½ cup	ketchup OR your favorite barbecue sauce	125 mL
2	garlic cloves, crushed	2

  *Moose, Goose & Things That Swim*

Barbecued Caribou Steak

Continued

1. Put the steaks in a glass or plastic dish, sprinkle liberally with the DLS* or seasoned salt and pepper.
2. Mix the soy sauce, vinegar, wine, sugar, ketchup and garlic.
3. Pour over the steaks and use a spoon or pastry brush to be sure all the steaks are well coated. Allow steaks to sit in the refrigerator or a cool place for at least 6 hours. You can leave them overnight if it is more convenient.
4. Barbecue over hot coals until desired doneness. Baste frequently with the marinade while cooking.

* *Dymond Lake Seasoning*

NOTE: *When doing a large batch of steaks you may have to double the marinade.*

The Care & Aging of Freshly Harvested Wild Game* (According to Doug Webber, Hunter Extraordinaire)

One year, when my girls were young, I was unable to "bring home the bacon." Roughly translated, this means that the great white hunter took a trip to the mobile meat market and got skunked! Upon hearing my tale of woe, my youngest daughter, Shari, then 4 years old, moaned, "Oh, no, this means we have to eat beef all winter!" And it was a hardship, for all of us had grown very fond of the lean but delicious wild meat that Helen had learned to cook so well, in such a variety of ways. But her cooking skills are only partly responsible for the high degree of acceptance of any wild fare that finds its way to our home. The other reason is the due care and attention I give to all my wild meat. I am very particular about keeping the meat as clean as possible, right from the very first slit of the skinning knife to the last wrap of the butcher paper. The only other step in my butchering process is to hang the meat for 3 to 20 days – the length of time being determined by the cut of meat and the temperature of the cold room.

An average temperature would be 40-50°F (4.4-10°C). I hang the ribs for only 3 days; the backbone with only an inch or so of rib I hang for a week; the front hangs for 3 days if it is being ground up, and 10 days if it is being cut into steaks and roasts; the hind quarters hang for 20 days. During the hanging time, dry skin will form on the meat, and occasionally bits of mold form as well. Don't worry about the mold, it gets trimmed off with the dry skin.

A quick way to age a roast is to leave it uncovered on a plate in a cool room, 60°F (15.5°C) for up to a week. If it smells a bit or ends up with mold on it, simply take a half and half water and vinegar solution and wash it well, rinsing with clear water – and presto – a cut fit for the most discriminating palate.

I leave my steak meat in roast-size chunks and cut it just prior to cooking, after it has reached room temperature. It is more tender this way. I caution you, however, not to overcook a tender cut; even wild meat is at its best if the middle is rare to medium.(This does not apply to bear!)

* *My experience is with moose, caribou and deer.*

Rack of Caribou

(HELEN) The first time we served this was at the Manitoba Chamber of Commerce Annual Convention in Churchill in April 1995. The caribou had been supplied by the Keewatin Development Board and my brother-in-law, Gavin, (whom those of you who have our first book "Blueberries & Polar Bears" will have read about) agreed to be in charge of the cooking. If I tell you that the 100 or so people who attended the dinner gave Gavin a standing ovation for the caribou that should say it all! A number of the people from the Keewatin told us that in all the years they had lived in the North they had never had caribou taste so good. The recipe is surprisingly easy; be sure to try it with other wild meats.

2	garlic cloves, crushed	2
2	racks* caribou, deer OR antelope	2
	DLS** OR salt and pepper	
½ lb.	salt pork, cut in strips, OR bacon	250 g
2 tbsp.	cooking oil	30 mL
2 tbsp.	butter OR margarine	30 mL
1½ oz.	pkg. onion soup mix	40 g
1 cup	beef stock	250 mL
½ cup	water	125 mL
1½ cups	sliced mushrooms, OR 10 oz. (284 mL) can	375 mL

1. Rub the crushed garlic clove on both sides of the racks and sprinkle liberally with the DLS** or salt and pepper.
2. Heat the oil, butter and a small chunk of the salt pork in a heavy frying pan.
3. Brown the racks on both sides in the oil mixture.
4. Remove the racks to a shallow baking pan. Lay strips of the salt pork over them.
5. Roast in a 350°F (180°C) oven for approximately 45 minutes-1 hour, until they have reached the desired doneness. Medium to medium rare is best.
6. Remove racks from the pan, cut in half; place on a serving platter and keep warm. Add the drippings from the pan plus the onion soup mix, stock, water and mushrooms to the drippings in the frying pan. Bring to a boil and simmer for 5 minutes.
7. Pour a small amount of the pan gravy over the racks. Serve the rest in a gravy boat.

Serves 4.

SERVING SUGGESTION: *This teams up well with Marie's Wild Rice Casserole, "Blueberries & Polar Bears", page 126 and Broccoli and Onion Au Gratin, page 139, in this book.*

* *A rack is a portion of the rib section, usually containing about 8 ribs.*
** *Dymond Lake Seasoning*

See photograph on page 17.

Moose, Goose & Things That Swim

Sweet 'N' Sour Caribou Steaks

This works well with deer, moose or elk also.

8	caribou steaks	8
3 tbsp.	olive OR vegetable oil	45 mL
2 tsp.	DLS* OR 1 tsp. (5 mL) salt and ½ tsp. (2 mL) pepper	10 mL
1½ cups	brown sugar	375 mL
2 tsp.	prepared mustard	10 mL
2 tbsp.	vinegar	30 mL

1. Brown the meat in the oil in a heavy skillet over medium-high heat. Place in an ovenproof casserole or roaster. If the steaks don't fit in a single layer, just be sure to put the sauce between the layers.
2. Cover and roast at 350°F (180°C) for 1 hour. You may have to increase cooking time if using moose or elk steaks.

Serves 8.

Onion-Smothered Deer Steak

(Helen) When my daughter Shari married David, we not only gained another son but a whole collection of family recipes to try. This is one that David's dad, Larry, has served us and we have thoroughly enjoyed it. Remember you can substitute moose, elk, caribou or antelope.

8	deer steaks	8
2	garlic cloves, crushed	2
	oil for frying	
	DLS* OR salt and pepper	
1	large onion, sliced in rings	1
2 cups	beef stock	500 mL
¼ cup	flour	60 mL
1 cup	water	250 mL

1. Rub steaks with crushed garlic, then sprinkle with DLS* or salt and pepper on both sides and allow to sit for 15 minutes.
2. Brown in oil in a heavy frying pan and move to a shallow dish. Spread onion over the steaks and pour over the beef stock.
3. Cover and bake at 350°F (180°C) for 1 hour, or until tender.
4. Remove the steaks from the pan and keep warm.
5. Mix flour and water to a smooth paste, add to the pan juices, bring to a boil and simmer until thickened. Adjust the seasoning and serve with the steaks. These are great with Garlicky Mashed Potatoes, page 133, and Nifty Carrots, page 136.

Serves 4.

* *Dymond Lake Seasoning*

Deer Sausage

This recipe came to us through one of our trusty guides, Mike Boll. Mike comes to us from Saskatchewan and has proven himself to be one of our greatest assets. Not only is he a first-class hunting and fishing guide, but he is also a first-class cabinet maker which is in evidence in his carpentry work around the lodge. And on top of all that he is a real nice guy!

He is one of those people who takes everything in his stride and keeps smiling! So, with this recipe, you will see that along with all his other great attributes, he can make a mean sausage. (He usually uses deer meat but, since that is nonexistent in our area, we substitute caribou or moose. You try whatever you can get your hands on.) Oh, and just one other point, Mike says that these turn out much better if you have a pitcher of Margarita's on hand when you are mixing them up!

12 lbs.	caribou, moose OR deer OR whatever you have	5.5 kg
12 lbs.	pork*	5.5 kg
4 cups	water	1 L
6 tbsp.	salt	90 mL
¼ cup	pepper	60 mL
½ cup	brown sugar	125 mL
4	large garlic cloves, crushed	4
	sausage casing	

1. Using the coarse blade on your grinder, grind up the wild meat and pork with the water. (Mike advises that if you grind it too fine it will have the consistency of wieners.)
2. In a large container, using your hands unless you have a new cement mixer, mix the ground meat with the rest of the ingredients.
3. Using your sausage maker according to the instructions, make your sausages.
4. Now, at this point, you can package them and freeze them or, if you wish, you can smoke them for a couple of hours first.
5. To serve, allow sausages to thaw and then either sauté until cooked through or put them on a baking tray and bake in the oven at 350°F (180°C) for 30 minutes.

Makes 24 lbs. (11 kg) of sausages.

* *Be sure that the pork contains some fat, as wild meat is very lean.*

Goose Facts – How Big Is A Canada Goose?

There are actually 10 sub-species, all wearing the famous neckband. They range in size from the pint-sized Cackling Goose, weighing in at 3 lbs., to the Giant Canada which has been known to reach 24 lbs. and have a wingspan of 75" (483 cm).

Moose, Goose & Things That Swim

Red Wine and Garlic Moose Roast

You can throw this great meat and gravy recipe in the pot early in the day, go about your business and come back to find a wonderful aroma filling your house. We have called for a moose roast but you can use elk, deer or caribou.

4-6 lb.	moose roast	2-2.5 kg
½ cup	red wine vinegar	125 mL
2	garlic cloves, crushed	2
2 tbsp.	salt	30 mL
1 cup	dry red wine	250 mL
	cold water	
½ cup	flour	125 mL
1 tbsp.	DLS* OR 1 tsp. (5 mL) salt and ½ tsp. (2 mL) pepper	15 mL
2	garlic cloves, crushed	2
2 tbsp.	brown sugar	30 mL
1 tsp.	prepared mustard, American OR Dijon	5 mL
1 tbsp.	Worcestershire sauce	15 mL
¼ cup	red wine vinegar OR lemon juice	60 mL
1 cup	dry red wine	250 mL
1	large onion, sliced	1
14 oz.	can tomatoes, crushed OR diced	398 mL

1. Place the roast in a plastic or glass container, large enough so that you will be able to completely cover the roast with the marinade.
2. Combine vinegar, garlic, salt and wine. Add water to completely cover the roast. Cover and marinate in the refrigerator overnight.
3. Mix the flour and DLS*. Remove the roast from the marinade and roll in the flour mixture. Brown in 2 tbsp. (30 mL) of oil in a heavy skillet over medium-high heat.
4. Place the roast in a slow cooker or heavy roaster.
5. Mix the remaining garlic cloves, brown sugar, mustard, Worcestershire, vinegar, wine, onion slices and tomatoes. Pour over the roast.
6. Cover and cook on low in a slow cooker for 10-12 hours, or in the oven at 250°F (120°C) for 6 hours.

Serves 8-10.

* Dymond Lake Seasoning

Goose Facts – How Old Is A Tough Old Bird??

The recorded ages of banded birds vary from 12 to 80 years! One captive pair was known to have been mated for 42 years!

Moose Stroganoff

You can use wild meat in anything that calls for beef. Serve over egg noodles with a crisp green salad. Crusty Brown Buns, page 60, are a nice addition too.

2 lbs.	moose sirloin steak (caribou, elk OR deer), cut into ½ x 2" (1.3 x 5 cm) strips	1 kg
¼ cup	flour	60 mL
¼ cup	vegetable oil	60 mL
1	large onion, thinly sliced	1
1½ cups	sliced mushrooms OR 10 oz. (284 mL) can, drained	375 mL
2 tbsp.	flour	30 mL
1 cup	beef stock	250 mL
2 tbsp.	ketchup	30 mL
1 tbsp.	Worcestershire sauce	15 mL
½ tsp.	dry mustard	2 mL
2 tsp.	DLS* or 1 tsp. (5 mL) salt and ½ tsp. (2 mL) pepper or more to taste	10 mL
1 cup	sour cream	250 mL
3 tbsp.	sherry (optional)	45 mL

1. Dredge the steak strips in the flour.
2. Heat the oil in a heavy skillet. Add the steak strips in batches and sauté, turning to brown on all sides. Remove sautéed strips and keep warm. Repeat until all steak is cooked.
3. Place all meat in skillet; add the onions and mushrooms and cook over medium heat until tender. Remove the meat and onions from the pan.
4. Blend in the flour, stock, ketchup, Worcestershire, mustard and DLS*, stirring constantly until smooth and thickened.
5. Return the meat and onion to the pan. Add the sour cream and sherry. Heat thoroughly but do not allow to boil.

Serves 6-8.

Madeira Game Sauce À La Rebhun

Dan Rebhun has hunted with us at Dymond Lake a number of times and we thank him for this recipe. It is super with wild goose, venison, moose or any game!

14 oz.	can purple plums, drained	398 mL
6 tbsp.	butter OR margarine	90 mL
1 tsp.	EACH dried onion, dry mustard, ground ginger	5 mL
2 tbsp.	lemon juice	30 mL
2 tbsp.	chili sauce	30 mL
¼ cup	Madeira (Portuguese fortified wine)	60 mL

  Moose, Goose & Things That Swim

Madeira Game Sauce À La Rebhun

Continued

1. Remove the pits from the plums and purée the plums in a blender.
2. Combine the plums with the butter, onion, mustard, ginger, lemon juice and chili sauce in a heavy saucepan. Simmer for 30 minutes.
3. Add the wine, remove from the heat.
4. Serve over or under any wild game, or with Duck Liver Pâté, page 16.

Makes about 1½ cups (375 mL).

Goose Liver Mousse

(HELEN) This is another wonderful recipe from Toni's mother-in-law, Gail. It is great to be able to share our love of cooking as well as our love of our mutual children and grandchildren!

½ cup	butter, softened	250 mL
1	shallot OR small onion, finely chopped	1
½ lb.	goose livers, trimmed* OR chicken liver	250 g
	DLS** OR salt and freshly ground pepper	
½ tsp.	dried thyme	2 mL
2 tbsp.	cognac OR white wine	30 mL
¾ cup	whipping cream	175 mL

1. Melt 2-3 tbsp. (30-45 mL) of the butter in a heavy skillet on medium. Add the onions and cook until soft but not colored.
2. Increase heat and add the livers. Sauté rapidly, seasoning with the DLS**or salt and pepper and the thyme. When livers are gray on the outside but still rare, add the cognac and cook another few minutes.
3. Cool slightly and then press through a fine, firm sieve, a bit at a time. Add the rest of the butter as you go along. You will have a warm, slightly liquid purée.
4. Whip the cream until is is semifirm but pourable and stir it into the liver purée. The cream must not be stiffly beaten or the mousse will be dry and cottony rather than firm, moist and velvety. Pour the mousse into a small serving bowl or mold.
5. Chill well before serving. The mousse will keep 2-3 days if covered with plastic wrap or a thin layer of melted butter. Serve with baguette slices or Melba toast.

Makes about 3 cups (750 mL) of mousse.

* *To trim livers, cut in half and remove any fat and any veins. Cut away any yellowy fiber as this is from the gall and it is bitter.*
** *Dymond Lake Seasoning*

Duck Liver Pâté

The rich flavors of duck or goose livers make this creamy pâté irresistible.

2 tbsp.	butter	30 mL
½ cup	minced onion	125 mL
½ lb.	duck, goose OR chicken livers	250 g
1 cup	chicken stock	250 mL
4	hard-cooked eggs	4
1 cup	cooked duck meat	250 mL
2 tsp.	Dijon mustard	10 mL
6 drops	Tabasco sauce	6 drops
1	garlic clove, crushed	1
3 tbsp	brandy	45 mL
2 tbsp	lemon juice	30 mL
	salt and pepper OR DLS*	
⅔ cup	butter	150 mL
¼ lb.	cooked ham, finely diced	115 g
½ cup	pecans, finely ground	125 mL

1. Melt 2 tbsp. (30 mL) butter in a small frying pan. Add onion and sauté until soft.
2. Simmer livers in stock for 5 minutes. Drain.
3. In a blender or food processor, purée onion, livers, eggs, duck meat, mustard, Tabasco, garlic, brandy and lemon juice until absolutely smooth.
4. Force pâté through a sieve to remove all fibers. Season with salt and pepper or DLS*. Add remaining butter and purée until completely blended.
5. Add ham and mix, but do not purée. Refrigerate, covered, overnight.
6. For individual servings, line large muffin tins with paper baking cups. Fill cups with pâté. Refrigerate overnight. To serve, unmold individual pâtés on small plates. Top with pecans.

Serves 12 OR makes 12 small pâté molds.

* *Dymond Lake Seasoning*

SERVING SUGGESTION: Spoon a pool of Madiera Game Sauce, page 14, on each plate and place pâté on top of sauce.

See photograph on page 121.

Wild Game – Caribou

Rack of Caribou, page 10
Sweet and Sour Baked Beans, page 136
Pepper Side Dish, page 141

  Moose, Goose & Things That Swim

Wild Duck Casserole

2	ducks	2
	DLS* OR salt and pepper to taste	
2 tbsp.	butter, melted	30 mL
1	medium turnip	1
4	bacon slices, cut into strips	4
1½ cups	sliced or quartered mushrooms OR 10 oz. (284 mL) can	375 mL
2 tbsp.	brandy	30 mL
¼ cup	game-bird stock OR chicken stock	60 mL

1. Preheat oven to 450°F (230°C)
2. Rub ducks inside and out with DLS*. Brush with melted butter. Roast in the oven for 40 minutes, basting occasionally with butter. Remove birds and set aside on a plate.
3. Peel and cube turnip. Cook for 5 minutes in salted water, drain.
4. Fry bacon over medium-high heat. Once bacon starts to get crisp, add mushrooms and fry for a few minutes. Remove with a slotted spoon.
5. Lower oven to 375°F (190°C). Cut off duck legs and breasts and place in an ovenproof 1½-quart (1.5 L) casserole. Pour brandy, stock and pan juices over meat; add turnip, bacon and mushrooms. Cover and place in the oven for 30 minutes, or until meat is tender.
6. Serve in the casserole and complement it with a salad.

Serves 4.

* *Dymond Lake Seasoning*

Goose Facts – Home Sweet Home

Canada Geese are found from Mexico to the Arctic and from the Atlantic to the Pacific, but a mated pair returns to the same nesting spot year after year. That may be on the tundra or in fields, in trees or on cliffs – as long as there is water nearby! They will accept man-made nests or reuse abandoned nests built by other birds, such as crows or hawks. One of their favorite nesting sites is on top of a muskrat lodge or beaver dam. They use whatever materials are close at hand, and the female lines the nest with down from her own breast. The gander defends the nesting area and he determines how large that area will be.

Float plane at the dock at North Knife Lake.

Duck à l'Orange

Roast duck is a little tricky as you have to be careful that it doesn't dry out. The most important thing is to choose a young bird with a good layer of fat under its skin. Keeping it covered, basting and not overcooking are also important.

2	plucked ducks OR 1 small plucked goose	2
1	medium onion, quartered	1
2 tsp.	DLS* OR 1 tsp. (5 mL) salt and ½ tsp. (2 mL) pepper	10 mL
¾ cup	currant jelly	175 mL
⅓ cup	white sugar	75 mL
1 tbsp.	grated orange rind	15 mL
¼ cup	port wine	60 mL
¼ cup	orange juice	60 mL
½ tsp.	salt	2 mL
	dash of cayenne pepper	
¼ cup	lemon juice	60 mL

1. Place ducks or goose on sheets of aluminum foil that are large enough to completely wrap around the birds and seal. One sheet for each duck.
2. Place the onions in the bird cavity and sprinkle liberally with DLS*.
3. Wrap the foil around the birds and fold over to seal.
4. Roast at 500°F (260°C) for 20 minutes (30 minutes for goose).
5. In a small saucepan, combine the jelly, sugar, orange rind, port, orange juice, salt and cayenne. Simmer for 5 minutes, remove from the heat and add the lemon juice.
6. Peel back the foil and brush the bird with the glaze. Reseal and return the bird to the oven until done, approximately 10 minutes (20 minutes for goose). Open the foil and use the juices to baste the bird again, at least once during the remaining baking time.

Serves 3.

SERVING SUGGESTIONS: Serve with Cranberry Sauce, page 198 "Blueberries & Polar Bears", or Cranberry Orange Relish, page 199.

* *Dymond Lake Seasoning*

See photograph on page 155.

World's Shortest Grace – "Heavenly Pa, Ta!"

Mushroom, Wild Rice and Goose Casserole

(HELEN) I am not too sure how this recipe was missed from "Blueberries & Polar Bears". It was and still is a favorite of my daughter Jeannie's. Just add a salad, some cranberry sauce and dinner is ready.

2	whole geese (actually, you can use ducks also OR just a pot full of legs OR a combination of both)	2
¾ cup	butter OR margarine	175 mL
1 cup	chopped onion	250 mL
1 cup	chopped celery	250 mL
3 cups	sliced mushrooms OR 2 x 10 oz. (284 mL) cans	750 mL
2 tsp.	DLS* or 1 tsp. (5 mL) salt and ½ tsp. (2 mL) pepper	10 mL
½ cup	flour	125 mL
3 cups	milk	750 mL
4 cups	cooked, wild rice	1 L
¼ cup	broth from goose	60 mL

1. Cover the goose or duck with water and simmer until the meat falls off the bone. Remove the meat, cool and dice. Save ¼ cup (60 mL) of broth.
2. Melt butter in a large Dutch oven, add onion, celery and mushrooms and cook until translucent. Add flour and stir until smooth. Slowly add milk and cook until thickened. Remove from the heat and add the remainder of the ingredients.
3. Pour into a greased 3-quart (3 L) casserole and bake at 325°F (160°C) for 1 hour.

Serves 4-6.

* *Dymond Lake Seasoning*

Goose Facts – The Mother Goose Nursery

Eggs are laid anywhere from early March in the U.S. to early June in the Arctic. The female goose lays one egg every other day until her clutch is formed – up to twelve eggs, but five to eight is normal. The first eggs are simply camouflaged – it doesn't matter if they get cold. Halfway through the laying, she will start to line her nest with down from her own breast for insulation. Only when all the eggs are laid will she start incubating, so that all the eggs will hatch at the same time – 28 or 29 days later. The female stays on the nest all time, except for a few outings for food and water: therefore she can lose a lot of weight during the incubation period. The male stays close to defend the nest, but otherwise does not assist his mate.

Goose Stir-Fry

Serve this to guests and they will have a hard time believing it is not a beef stir-fry! We have suggested some vegetables here but don't be afraid to substitute or add a few. Cooking after all is an ever changing art!

6	medium goose breasts	6
1 cup	soy sauce	250 mL
2	garlic cloves, crushed	2
	vegetable oil	
1 cup	chunked onions	250 mL
½ cup	chunked celery	125 mL
1 cup	broccoli florets	250 mL
1 cup	cauliflower florets	250 mL
1	green pepper cut in strips	1
1 cup	diagonally-cut carrots	250 mL
1 cup	sliced mushrooms	250 mL
2 tbsp.	fresh ginger root, chopped (optional)	30 mL
3 tbsp.	cornstarch	45 mL
½ cup	cold water	125 mL
	DLS* OR salt and pepper to taste	

1. Cut the goose breasts into long thin strips and place in a glass or plastic bowl. Add the soy sauce and crushed garlic. Stir well, cover and place in the refrigerator to marinate 6-8 hours or even overnight.
2. Remove goose from marinade and drain slightly; reserve the marinade.
3. Heat 2 tbsp. (30 mL) of oil in a large heavy skillet or wok. Add ½ the goose and stir-fry over medium-high heat, until nicely browned. Remove from the pan, add a bit more oil and fry the second batch of goose. Remove from the pan.
4. Wipe out the pan and add 2 tbsp. (30 mL) of oil. Now, stir-fry the vegetables and ginger until tender-crisp, about 7 minutes.
5. When vegetables are tender-crisp, return the goose to the pan and add the reserved marinade. Cook over medium heat until just simmering.
6. Meanwhile, mix the cornstarch with the water and add to the saucepan. Stir gently until the sauce thickens and loses its cloudiness. Season to taste.

Serves 6.

SERVING SUGGESTION: *This is delicious served over a bed of noodles or rice.*

* *Dymond Lake Seasoning*

Mandarin Goose

Wild goose is a delicious dark meat that can be substituted for beef or in some chicken dishes. This recipe is especially good. Team it up with a rice dish, a mixed green salad, crusty French bread and you'll have a winner.

12	tender (young) goose breasts	12
½-1 cup	flour	125-250 mL
1 tsp.	DLS* OR ½ tsp. (2 mL) salt and ¼ tsp. (1 mL) pepper	5 mL
4-6 tbsp.	vegetable oil	60-90 mL
10 oz.	can mandarin oranges	284 mL
⅓ cup	soy sauce	75 mL
¼ cup	brown sugar	60 mL
½ tsp.	ground mace	2 mL
2 tbsp.	vegetable oil	30 mL
½ cup	chunked green pepper	125 mL
½ cup	chunked red pepper	125 mL
1 cup	chunked onion	250 mL
½ cup	chunked celery	125 mL
1 cup	sliced OR button mushrooms	250 mL

1. Cut the goose breasts into ¾" (1.8 cm) chunks (approximately 4 cups [1 L]). Shake in a mixture of the flour and DLS*.
2. Heat 4 tbsp. (60 mL) of oil in a heavy skillet. Add goose pieces about a third at a time and brown. Remove to a 9 x 13" (23 x 33 cm) OR 3-quart (3 L) casserole as they are done. Add more oil, if needed.
3. Drain the oranges and mix the juice with the soy sauce, brown sugar and mace. Pour this mixture over the goose pieces and bake, uncovered, at 350°F (180°C) for 45 minutes, stirring once.
4. While the goose is in the oven, wipe out the skillet and add the additional 2 tbsp. (30 mL) of oil. Add the vegetables and stir-fry until tender-crisp, about 5 minutes.
5. After 45 minutes, remove goose from oven; gently stir in oranges and vegetables. Return to oven for another 15 minutes.

Serves 6-8.

* *Dymond Lake Seasoning*

Goose Facts – "Till Death Do Us Part"

When a goose gets sick or wounded and falls out of formation, two other geese fall out and follow it down to give help and protection. They stay with the fallen goose, often at their own peril until it dies or is able to fly again.

Moose, Goose & Things That Swim

Goose à la Cherry Sauce

We are always on the lookout for new wild goose recipes and this one comes to us via a friend of Marie's whose name is Mary DYMOND. She is the first person we have met in our twenty-eight years of running Dymond Lake Lodge whose name has the same spelling. We knew the recipe would be a winner. Long, slow cooking makes this recipe a good one for the big Canada's or older geese.

4	large goose breasts	4
1 cup	flour	250 mL
	oil for browning	
2 cups	beef stock	500 mL
2 tbsp.	A-1 OR HP sauce	30 mL
¼ cup	sherry	60 mL
⅛ tsp.	dried marjoram OR ½ tsp. (2 mL) fresh	0.5 mL
2 tsp.	DLS* OR 1 tsp. (5 mL) salt and ½ tsp. (2 mL) pepper	10 mL
2	bay leaves	2
2 tbsp.	cornstarch	30 mL
14 oz.	can sweet pitted cherries, drained, juice saved	398 mL
2 tbsp.	brandy	30 mL

1. Cut goose breasts into chunks, like stewing beef. Dredge in flour and brown in the oil in a Dutch oven. Remove the goose to a bowl.
2. To the drippings in the Dutch oven, add the beef stock, A-1 or HP sauce, sherry, marjoram, DLS* and bay leaves. Simmer for 2-3 minutes, add the goose, cover and cook in a 325°F (160°C) oven for 2½ hours, or until goose is tender.
3. Mix the cornstarch with about ¼ cup (60 mL) of the cherry juice. Stir until smooth and then add the rest of the juice and the brandy.
4. Remove the pan from the oven and remove the meat. Add the cornstarch mixture and cook over medium heat until thickened and bubbly. Add the goose and simmer for 15 minutes. Add the cherries and remove from the heat. Serve with rice or pasta.

Serves 8.

* *Dymond Lake Seasoning*

Goose Facts – Geese Are Only Human!

We've all been taught that geese mate for life, and that may be true if both live to a ripe old age. But most geese will remate after a partner's death, sometimes within days. And, divorce will occasionally occur as well.

Drambuie Goose

This recipe came to us via our friends Hank and Berry from Australia. They came to Churchill for a visit a couple of years ago and Hank brought a number of recipes with him. This was originally a chicken recipe but we decided to try it with wild goose and it was definitely a "keeper".

8	medium goose breasts, skinned, boneless	8
½ cup	flour	125 mL
2 tsp	DLS* OR ½ tsp. (2 mL) salt and ½ tsp. (2 mL) pepper	10 mL
¼ cup	butter OR margarine	60 mL
2	garlic cloves, crushed	2
2 cups	strong chicken stock	500 mL
6	shallots OR 1 medium onion, finely chopped	6
1 cup	half and half cream	250 mL
2 tbsp.	Drambuie liqueur	30 mL
2 tsp.	chopped parsley	10 mL

1. Pound each breast until thin; a rolling pin or wine bottle works well for this. Cut the pieces in half if the pounding makes them quite large.
2. Dredge the meat in the flour and seasoning mixture.
3. Sauté the goose in the butter over medium heat until nicely browned. Remove from the pan. Add more butter, if needed.
4. Leave about 1 tbsp. (15 mL) of butter in the pan. Add the garlic and sauté for 2 minutes. Add the chicken stock and bring to a boil. Return the goose to the pan, cover and simmer gently until the goose is tender, 30-40 minutes.
5. Remove the goose from the pan and add the shallots or onions. Cook until they are translucent, approximately 5 minutes. Add the cream, Drambuie and parsley; simmer until the sauce thickens slightly, about 5 minutes again! Return the goose to the pan; stir to coat with the sauce and to heat through.

Serves 4.

SERVING SUGGESTION: This is great with Saffron Rice, page 131, Pepper Side Dish, page 141, and our Egyptian Salad, page 119.

* *Dymond Lake Seasoning*

Marinated Cold-Smoked Lake Trout
— Lemon Pepper or Orange Sugar

Eric Bromberg, who is co-owner and one of the chefs at the Blue Ribbon Cafe in New York, showed us how to make this wonderful hors d'oeuvre. Not only that, he instructed Stewart on how to make a new, improved smoker. The results were spectacular and this became the favorite of the season.

> **lake trout fillets, skin on**
> **salt**
> **freshly diced lemon rind**
> **freshly ground pepper**
> **brown sugar**

Lemon Pepper:

> **freshly diced lemon rind**
> **freshly ground pepper**

Orange Sugar:

> **freshly diced orange peel**
> **brown sugar**

1. You will need a pan, with sides, that is long enough to lay out the fish fillet. Sprinkle the pan generously with salt. Lay out the fish fillet, skin-side down. Sprinkle generously with finely diced lemon rind and freshly ground pepper. Sprinkle generously with salt.
2. Let fish sit overnight in refrigerator. Drain fish. Sprinkle generously with brown sugar. Turn skin-side up. Prepare salt brine (below) and pour it over the fish.
3. *Salt Brine:* Saturate cool water with salt and mix until salt won't dissolve any more. (When Eric showed us how to do this, he just kept adding salt to a big bowl of cool water and mixing it with his hand until the salt started collecting on the bottom of the bowl and wouldn't dissolve any more. Then he poured the liquid carefully over the fish, leaving the undissolved salt in the bottom of the bowl.) We are talking a lot of salt here!
4. Let fish soak for 4 hours. Rinse fish. Soak fish in fresh water for ½ hour. Drain and pat fish dry. Refrigerate the fish, uncovered, overnight.
5. Press into fish: **freshly diced lemon peel and freshly ground pepper OR freshly diced orange peel and brown sugar.**
6. Cold-smoke the filets for 2-3 hours. When the fish comes out of the smoker, any protruding bones should be removed immediately, without disturbing the fish. (Strong tweezers work well.)
7. Refrigerate, uncovered, if fish is going to be used the same day. To keep for future use, brush the filet with olive oil, and wrap in plastic wrap. Refrigerate for up to 2 weeks.

  Moose, Goose & Things That Swim

Cold-Smoked Lake Trout Hors d'Oeuvres*:

> cold-smoked lake trout
> firm brown bread OR rye OR pumpernickel
> cream cheese OR sour cream
> chopped fresh chives OR finely chopped red onion

1. Thinly slice the fish on an angle, across the back, towards the tail.
2. Prepare thin slices of firm brown bread by spreading with a thin layer of cream cheese or sour cream. Arrange a thin slice of fish on the bread. Sprinkle with chopped fresh chives.

Cold-Smoked Lake Trout Cornets*:

8 oz.	cream cheese	250 g
2 tbsp.	capers, with juice	30 mL
¼	fresh lemon, squeezed	¼
1 tbsp.	fresh chives	15 mL
	thinly sliced cold smoked lake trout	

1. Combine cream cheese, capers with juice, lemon juice and chives. Roll a slice of fish around a small spoonful of the cheese mixture. Secure with a toothpick (optional). Serve.

* *If Cold Smoked Lake Trout is not available, try these recipes with smoked salmon or lox, or the Marinated Lake Trout on page 38.*

See photograph on page 35.

Cold Smoking – Another Dissertation by Doug

Cold smoking your favorite fish is a sure way to win rave reviews from even the most discriminating of guests. Follow one of the recipes for marinating fish in brine (Blueberries & Polar Bears, page 26, OR Cranberries & Canada Geese, page 26) then proceed with the smoking process. With cold smoking the fire needs to be a good distance away from the smoker (a minimum of 4' [1.2 m]) The fire container is joined to the smoker by a length of 3-6" (7-15 cm) pipe. My smoker is made from a 45 gallon (204 L) drum with a hinged lid mid section. (See picture, page 36.) A 6' (1.82 m) length of 3" (7 cm) pipe connects it to a 10 gallon (45 L) drum that houses the coals and shavings. (You can also use a small propane burner turned down very low under a large pan of the shavings and chips.) I use red willow, hickory, apple and cherry wood or any combination of the above. A small fire covered with damp sawdust and chips works well, and with a bit of practice can be kept just smoldering instead of actually burning. A minimum of 4 hours up to 12 hours in the smoker will produce a fine, high-quality product. The smoker should always be cool to the touch. Trout and whitefish work very well for us in the north but any fish will do. Just slab it and leave the skin and bones on. Put the marinated slab, skin side down, on the racks or, if your smoker is an upright model, don't cut the slab all the way through at the tail, just drape the whole fish over the rod or section of the rack.

When the fish is smoked to your liking, brush it well with olive oil, wrap it in plastic wrap and store it in the refrigerator. It will keep for 2 weeks – longer if frozen.

Golden Caviar

As we have told you in the introduction, we did the pictures for this book on location at North Knife Lake. While we were doing the pictures, our good friend, Jim, from Santa Barbara was doing a bit (understatement) of fishing. When he walked into the kitchen with a handful of trout roe, we had to confess that we had never really done much with trout roe in the past and being up to our ears in shots for the book, this didn't seem to be the time to start. Margo, our food stylist, had other ideas though. She just took those eggs and next thing we knew – well, in all honesty, it is a fairly time consuming job – we had "Golden Caviar". It not only looked lovely, it tasted superb!

Removing all the eggs from the membrane has to be done by hand and very carefully – a few broken eggs won't be missed! As you peel the eggs off of the membrane, put them into cold water. They may look completely clean to you until you place them into the water and then you will often see a spot of membrane. Take them out and remove it. When you have them all clean, drain them in a strainer.

Golden Caviar*:

	lake trout roe	
1 cup	water	250 mL
1 tbsp.	salt	15 mL

Place roe in a brine of water and salt, making more brine if needed. Cover and refrigerate 24 hours; drain in a strainer. Gently run cold water over the eggs until they are very well rinsed. Put them out on paper towel and pat dry. At this point they are ready to be used in the following hors d'oeuvres:

Cream Cheese with Golden Caviar*:

8 oz.	cream cheese, softened	250 g
3 tbsp.	mayonnaise	45 mL
2-3	green onions, chopped	2-3
	Golden Caviar*	

Mix the cream cheese, mayonnaise and green onions. Spread on melba toast or crackers and top with Golden Caviar.

* If you lack the trout roe or the patience to prepare Golden Caviar, substitute commercial whitefish or salmon caviar.

See photograph on page 155.

Moose, Goose & Things That Swim

Egg and Caper Spread with Golden Caviar:

3	eggs, hard-cooked	3
3 tbsp.	mayonnaise	45 mL
2 tsp.	DLS* OR 1 tsp. (5 mL) salt and ½ tsp. (2 mL) pepper	10 mL
2 tsp.	capers	10 mL
	Golden Caviar	

Grate the eggs and mix with the mayonnaise, seasoning and capers. Spread on the melba toast or crackers and top with Golden Caviar.

Grated Egg with Golden Caviar:

eggs, hard-cooked
sour cream OR cream cheese
Golden Caviar

Grate the eggs. Spread a little sour cream or cream cheese over melba toast or thin slices of toasted French bread (baguette size). Top with grated egg and Golden Caviar.

Seviche

This is a refreshing Latin American-inspired appetizer. The lime juice "cooks" the fish; besides adding a wonderful flavor, it also makes it firm and opaque.

1 lb. +	mild, white-fleshed fish	500 g +
2 cups	lime juice	500 mL
1	green pepper, seeded and diced	1
3	medium, ripe tomatoes, peeled, seeded and diced	3
⅓ cup	olive oil	75 mL
¼ cup	white vinegar	60 mL
3 tbsp.	chopped fresh parsley OR 1½ tsp. (7 mL) dried	45 mL
1 tbsp.	chopped fresh oregano OR ½ tsp. (2 mL) dried	15 mL
¾ tsp.	salt	3 mL
⅓ tsp.	black pepper	2 mL
1 tsp.	Tabasco sauce	5 mL
5 tbsp.	sugar	75 mL
1	garlic clove, very finely minced	1

1. Cut fish in ½" (2 cm) pieces. Put it in a 1-quart (1 L) glass (NOT METAL) container and add lime juice. Mix well.
2. Prepare green pepper and tomatoes, as above. Add to fish along with all other ingredients. Mix well.
3. Cover and refrigerate. Mix every ½ hour for 2-3 hours. It will keep for a week under refrigeration but is at its best from the 2nd-4th days.
4. Serve as an appetizer on lettuce leaves or as a snack with crackers.

Makes 1 quart (1 L).

Landlocked Lobster

The very brief cooking time, at high heat, is the secret to the lobster-like texture of this fish.

½ cup	butter, melted	125 mL
2 tsp.	crushed fresh garlic	10 mL
1 tbsp.	chopped fresh parsley	15 mL
	northern pike OR a similar firm, white, fresh-water boneless fish fillet	

1. Mix warm, melted butter with garlic and parsley. Place in a small serving bowl, on a small serving plate.
2. Cut fish into strips, approximately 2" (5 cm) long. Drop fish into boiling, salted water, a few strips at a time, so water doesn't stop boiling. Boil 1 minute. Drain. Repeat with remaining strips.
3. Place warm fish on plate, surrounding the bowl of butter dip. Serve with toothpicks.

See photograph on page 121.

Honey Pickerel

Another scrumptious way to serve those delicious pickerel (walleye to our American friends). As we all know, the best way is right out of the water and into the frying pan at a shore lunch but this dish runs a close second.

1	egg	1
2 tsp.	honey	10 mL
2 cups	cracker crumbs	500 mL
½ tsp.	salt	2 mL
6	pickerel fillets, or any firm white-fleshed fish	6
⅓-½ cup	oil	75-125 mL
	lemon wedges	

1. Beat the egg and honey in a shallow bowl.
2. In a plastic bag, combine the cracker crumbs and salt.
3. Dip the fillets in the egg mixture first and then shake in the crumbs.
4. Heat oil in a heavy frying pan over medium heat and fry the fillets until they are golden brown, approximately 3-5 minutes per side.

Serves 4-6, unless they are hungry fishermen or hunters, then it will only serve half that many, so adjust accordingly.

Moose, Goose & Things That Swim

Barbecued Lake Trout
with Dill or A Bite

Gavin's imagination often runs away on him when he starts cooking and we all benefit from its wanderings. Since these recipes are so similar, I thought we would just present them as one so you can take your pick. Salmon or char will work just as well.

With Dill

1	garlic clove, crushed	1
1 tbsp.	chopped fresh dillweed, OR 1 tsp. (5 mL) dried	15 mL
1 tsp.	paprika	5 mL
3-4 lb.	lake trout, filleted, skin on	1.5-2 kg

1. Rub the garlic, dill and paprika into the flesh of the fish.
2. Allow to sit for 30 minutes.
3. Barbecue, skin-side down, until fish flakes easily.

With A Bite

2 tbsp.	teriyaki OR soy sauce	30 mL
1 tbsp.	lemon juice	15 mL
1 tsp.	horseradish	5 mL
2 tbsp.	brown sugar	30 mL
2 tbsp.	jalapeño juice	30 mL
2 tbsp.	barbecue sauce	30 mL
1 tbsp.	DLS* (optional – if you have it)	15 mL
3-4 lb.	lake trout, filleted, skin on	1.5-2 kg

1. Combine all ingredients, except fish, for the marinade. Pour into a shallow glass pan.
2. Add the fish fillets turning to coat both sides. Cover and let sit for 1 hour, turning every 15 minutes.
3. Barbecue, skin-side down, until fish flakes easily. Brush occasionally with the marinade while cooking.

Serves 4.

VARIATION: This marinade works very well on a thick moose or elk steak too. Just increase the teriyaki or soy sauce to ½ cup (125 mL) add ½ cup (125 mL) dry red wine as well.

Mushroom and Dill-Stuffed Lake Trout with Dill Sauce

Here is an elegant dish fit for your finest company! Equally good with salmon, you can also do it over the coals on a barbecue.

4-5 lb.	lake trout, dressed	2-2.2 kg
	DLS* OR salt and pepper	

Mushroom and Dill Stuffing:

2 tbsp.	butter OR margarine	30 mL
1 cup	sliced fresh mushrooms	250 mL
½ cup	chopped onions	125 mL
¼ cup	chopped celery	60 mL
2 cups	bread cubes, can be stale, but not dry crumbs	500 mL
1 tbsp.	chopped fresh parsley	15 mL
1 tbsp.	lemon juice	15 mL
½ tsp.	dried dillweed OR 2 tbsp. (30 mL) fresh	2 mL
¼ cup	pine nuts	60 mL
2 tsp.	DLS* OR 1 tsp. (5 mL) salt and ½ tsp. (2 mL) pepper	10 mL

1. Wash and dry the fish. Set on a piece of heavy-duty aluminum foil that is large enough to completely wrap the fish. Sprinkle with DLS* or salt and pepper inside and out.
2. Melt the butter in a skillet and add the mushrooms, onions and celery. Cook for 5 minutes, until onions are translucent.
3. Mix the bread cubes in a bowl with the parsley, lemon juice, dill, pine nuts and DLS*. Add the onion mixture and mix well.
4. Fill the cavity of the fish with the stuffing. Don't worry if a bit of the stuffing falls out.
5. Wrap the foil around the fish and fold over to seal along the long edge and the ends.
6. Bake fish at 450°F (230°C) for approximately 35-40 minutes, turning once. The fish is done when the aroma starts to permeate the air. You want it to flake easily but still be firm and moist.
7. Serve with Dill Sauce, page 33.

Serves 4-6.

* *Dymond Lake Seasoning*

Dill Sauce

2 tbsp.	butter	30 mL
2 tbsp.	flour	30 mL
½ cup	dry white wine	125 mL
1 cup	half and half cream OR evaporated milk	250 mL
½ tsp.	salt	2 mL
1 tsp.	DLS* OR ½ tsp. (2 mL) pepper	5 mL
1 tbsp.	dried dillweed OR ¼ cup (60 mL) chopped fresh	15 mL
2	eggs, hard-boiled, finely chopped (optional)	2

1. Melt the butter over medium heat. Remove from the heat, stir in the flour and whisk until smooth.
2. Gradually add the white wine, cream, salt and DLS* or ¼ tsp. (1 mL) pepper, whisking until smooth.
3. Cook over medium heat, stirring constantly for 5 or 6 minutes, until thickened. If the sauce is too thick, add a bit more cream or some of the juices that have collected around the trout.
4. Stir in the dill and chopped egg, if desired.

Makes about 1½ cups (375 mL) of sauce.

Cajun Brook Trout

This very simple but delicious recipe can be used for rainbow trout, pickerel or any similar white-fleshed fish. It scores high in flavor but low in calories!

1½ tsp.	paprika	7 mL
¾ tsp.	pepper	3 mL
½ tsp.	EACH salt, dried oregano, chili powder and dry mustard	2 mL
¼ tsp.	dried thyme	1 mL
⅛ tsp.	cayenne pepper	0.5 mL
4	4 oz. (115 g) trout fillets	4
2 tsp.	vegetable oil	10 mL
2 tsp.	chopped fresh parsley	10 mL
1	green onion, chopped	1
	lemon wedges	

1. Combine the spices and herbs and set aside.
2. Pat fillets dry and place on a broiler rack. Lightly brush each side of fillets with oil; sprinkle both sides evenly with the paprika mixture.
3. Place the broiler rack 4-6" (10-15 cm) from the heat and broil for 4-5 minutes, until the fish flakes easily with a fork.
4. Place on a warm serving platter and sprinkle with the parsley and green onion. Garnish the platter with lemon wedges.

Serves 4

Crispy Fish with Lemon Caper Sauce

A golden fresh fish fillet is good anytime – with Lemon Caper Sauce, it is superb!

8	fish fillets, pike, pickerel OR other firm white fish	8
2 tbsp.	dry white vermouth	30 mL
1	bay leaf	1
6 tbsp.	olive oil	90 mL
½ cup	flour	125 mL
½ tsp.	salt	2 mL
½ tsp.	DLS* OR ¼ tsp. (1 mL) pepper	2 mL
2	eggs, lightly beaten	2
1½ cups	dry breadcrumbs	375 mL
	oil for frying	

Lemon Caper Sauce:

6 tbsp.	butter OR margarine	90 mL
1	garlic clove, crushed	1
2 tsp.	chopped fresh parsley OR ½ tsp. (2 mL) dried	10 mL
1 tsp.	chopped fresh oregano OR ⅓ tsp. (1.5 mL) dried	5 mL
2 tbsp.	chopped capers	30 mL
2 tbsp.	lemon juice	30 mL
	lemon and parsley for garnish	

1. Place the skinless, boneless fillets in a large, shallow nonmetal dish.
2. Combine the vermouth, bay leaf and oil in a saucepan and heat gently. Allow to cool completely and then pour over the fillets. Allow them to marinate for 1 hour, turning occasionally.
3. Mix the flour with salt and either DLS* or pepper. Remove the fish from the marinade and dredge with the flour.
4. Dip the fillets into the beaten egg then coat with breadcrumbs.
5. Heat ¼" (6 mm) of oil (no more) in a large frying pan. Add fillets and cook over medium heat until golden, about 3 minutes per side. Remove and drain on a wire rack; keep warm in a 150°F (70°C) oven.
6. Pour the oil out of the pan and wipe it clean. Add butter and garlic; cook until lightly browned. Add the herbs, capers and lemon juice.
7. Arrange the fillets on a serving tray and immediately pour over the herb butter. Garnish with lemon and parsley.

Serves 4.

* *Dymond Lake Seasoning*

Taste Teasers – Cold-Smoked Fish

Marinated Cold-Smoked Lake Trout – Lemon Pepper and Orange Sugar, page 26

Moose, Goose & Things That Swim

Lemon Butter Arctic Char

(HELEN) This recipe was gleaned from Gail Morberg, another young bride who found herself raising a family and cooking for a bunch of hungry fishermen at the same time. She did a great job of both (her son, Nelson, is my son-in-law). The buttery topping on this fish is sure to satisfy!

2	char fillets from a 4-5 lb. (1.8-2 kg) fish, (lake trout OR salmon will work too)	2
½ cup	soft butter	125 mL
2 tsp.	chopped fresh parsley	10 mL
1 tbsp.	finely chopped onion	15 mL
1	garlic clove, crushed (2 if they are small)	1
1 tsp.	lemon juice	5 mL
¼ tsp.	Tabasco sauce	1 mL
1 tbsp.	fine bread crumbs	15 mL
1 tsp.	DLS* OR ½ tsp. (2 mL) salt and ¼ tsp. (1 mL) pepper	5 mL

1. Remove the skin from the fillets.
2. Mix together the butter, parsley, onion, garlic, lemon juice, Tabasco, bread crumbs and DLS* or salt and pepper.
3. Place the fillets on a greased baking sheet or broiler pan. Broil on one side for 4 minutes.
4. Turn fillets over carefully and cover with the butter mixture.
5. Place under broiler and continue to broil for 3-4 minutes, until the fish flakes easily. Do not overcook or fish will be dry and flavorless.

Serves 4-6.

* *Dymond Lake Seasoning*

The Ichthyarian Creed

I believe in the power of fishing . . .
To afford me tranquil moments,
To restore my spirit,
To expose me to the wonders of nature,
To lend perspective to my existence,
And to kindle appreciation
For all I hold most precious.

Doug and Gary at the cold smoker – getting the fire going.

Insert – Marie and Helen checking the cold-smoked fish.

Marinated Lake Trout with Spruce Needles

Bruce Bromberg, co-owner of the Blue Ribbon Cafe in New York, made this for us when he was up in 1994. It was great fun watching him put everything together and a real eyebrow raiser when he sent Stewart out to get some branches off the spruce tree to throw in. They did add a nice subtle flavor!

4	lake trout fillets, skin on	4
1½ cups	rock salt	375 mL
½ cup	white sugar	125 mL
2 tbsp.	whole peppercorns, crushed	30 mL
2 tbsp.	fresh dillweed OR 2 tsp. (10 mL) dried	30 mL
⅛ tsp.	paprika	0.5 mL

Herb and Spice-Infused Oil Mixture:

2	small spruce ends, just the needle spikes	2
4 cups	olive oil	1 L
8	whole garlic cloves	8
1	small onion, cut in eights	1
2	bay leaves	2
1	whole clove	1
2 tbsp.	fresh dillweed OR 2 tsp. (10 mL) dried	30 mL
1 sprig	fresh fennel OR 1 tsp. (5 mL) dried	1 sprig
1 sprig	fresh tarragon OR 1 tsp. (5 mL) dried	1 sprig
1 tbsp.	pink peppercorns OR black	15 mL
⅛ tsp.	nutmeg	0.5 mL
½	red onion, cut in quarters	½
2	carrots, chopped	2

1. Lay fish fillets on a tray, skin side down.
2. Combine the salt, sugar, peppercorns, dill and paprika. Spread over the fillets. Cover with plastic wrap and refrigerate for 12 hours.
3. Prepare the oil mixture the day before also. Smash the spruce ends with a rolling pin or bottle to release flavor. Combine all the oil mixture ingredients in a heavy stockpot and heat over low until it reaches 80-85°F (27-30°C). It should never go over 100°F (37°C). This allows the herbs and spices to infuse the olive oil. When it reaches 80-85°F (27-30°C), remove from the heat, cover and let sit overnight.
4. After the fish has been refrigerated overnight, rinse well under cold water and dry with paper towel. Place the fillets on a clean tray and pour the oil mixture over. Use a pastry brush to be sure the fillets are well covered. Cover with plastic wrap and refrigerate for 12 hours.

Marinated Lake Trout with Spruce Needles

Continued

5. Remove the fillets from the refrigerator and turn them over. Using a pastry brush, pick up the oil mixture from the pan and coat the fillets. Replace the plastic wrap and refrigerate again. Repeat this procedure twice a day for the next 3 days. The fish is now ready to use.

SERVING SUGGESTION: Slice the fish from the head end towards the tail in thin slices on the bias. It is similar in texture to lox and can be used in the same manner. It can be used in the same hors d'oeuvres as the Marinated Cold-Smoked Lake Trout on page 27.

Herbed Baked Whole Fish

Herbed Sour Cream Sauce:

⅓ cup	chopped fresh basil, OR 1 tbsp. (15 mL) dried	75 mL
⅓ cup	chopped fresh parsley, lightly packed OR 1 tbsp. (15 mL) dried	75 mL
1	garlic clove	1
⅓ cup	olive oil	75 mL
	salt and ground black pepper	
½ cup	sour cream	125 mL
2 tbsp.	fresh rosemary OR 1 tsp. (5 mL) dried	30 mL
1	whole trout OR Arctic char about 4 lbs. (2 kg)	1
	lime slices	

1. Preheat oven to 350°F (180°C). Line a large baking pan with heavy-duty aluminum foil.
2. In a blender or food processor, purée basil, parsley and garlic with olive oil. Season the mixture with salt and pepper to taste.
3. Stir 2 tbsp. (30 mL) of herb mixture into the sour cream; cover and refrigerate the sauce until the fish is ready to serve.
4. Add rosemary to the remaining herb mixture and purée for 1 minute.
5. Using a sharp knife, make 3 shallow diagonal slashes on each side of the fish. Using your fingers, work the herb mixture into the slashes and cavity of the fish.
6. Place fish on prepared pan. Bake the fish, uncovered, until it flakes easily when tested with a fork, about 30 minutes.
7. Transfer the fish to a serving platter, and garnish with lime slices. Serve immediately with the chilled Herbed Sour Cream Sauce on the side.

Serves 4-6.

Baked Arctic Char Steaks

Arctic char is definitely the "King of the North" when it comes to fish. These recipes are equally good with lake trout or salmon.

4	1" (2.5 cm) thick char steaks	4
	DLS* or salt and pepper	
1½ cups	sliced fresh mushrooms OR 10 oz. (284 mL) can, drained	375 mL
1 tbsp.	lemon juice	15 mL
1 tbsp.	grated onion	15 mL
¼ cup	melted butter OR margarine	60 mL

1. Sprinkle steaks with DLS* or salt and pepper. Place in shallow, greased casserole.
2. Combine the mushrooms, lemon juice, onion and butter.
3. Pour over the steaks and bake at 350°F (180°C) for 30-35 minutes, until fish flakes easily.

Serves 4.

* *Dymond Lake Seasoning*

Broiled Char with Dijon Cream

Arctic Char can be found in either salt or fresh water and is a member of the salmon family. This recipe can be broiled or barbecued.

¾ cup	chicken stock	175 mL
½ cup	heavy cream	125 mL
2 tbsp.	Dijon mustard	30 mL
	DLS* OR salt and pepper	
4	6 oz. (170 g) char, salmon OR lake trout fillets	4
	lemon wedges	

1. Preheat the broiler or barbecue.
2. In a small saucepan, bring the stock and heavy cream to a boil over moderately high heat and simmer until reduced by half, about 5 minutes. Whisk in the mustard and DLS* or salt and pepper and bring just to a simmer. Cover and keep warm.
3. Sprinkle the fillets on both sides with DLS* or salt and pepper. Broil until just cooked through, about 4 minutes per side.
4. Transfer the fillets to warmed plates, spoon the sauce over the fish and serve with lemon wedges.

Serves 4.

* *Dymond Lake Seasoning*

Arctic Char or Trout Fillets au Gratin

This dish looks as good as it tastes. It is truly a "company dinner". Team it up with a wild rice dish and steamed broccoli and you are set. You can also use salmon for this recipe. Don't be afraid to substitute!

2 tbsp.	butter OR margarine	30 mL
¼ cup	finely chopped onion	60 mL
½ cup	finely chopped mushrooms	125 mL
2 tbsp.	finely chopped celery	30 mL
¼ cup	butter OR margarine	60 mL
¼ cup	flour	60 mL
1½ cups	milk	375 mL
1 tbsp.	lemon juice	15 mL
1 tsp.	DLS* OR ½ tsp. (2 mL) salt and ¼ tsp. (1 mL) pepper	5 mL
6	trout OR char fillets, approx. 6 oz. (170 g) each salt and pepper to taste	6
2 tbsp.	grated Parmesan cheese	30 mL
2 tbsp.	chopped fresh parsley	30 mL
6 tbsp.	grated medium Cheddar cheese	90 mL

1. Melt the 2 tbsp. (30 mL) of butter in a small frying pan and cook until the onions, mushrooms and celery are translucent. Do not allow them to brown. Set aside.
2. In a medium saucepan, over medium heat, melt ¼ cup (60 mL) butter; stir in the flour until well blended. Slowly add the milk, whisking constantly until the sauce comes to a boil and thickens. Gradually add the lemon juice; season with DLS* or salt and pepper. Stir in the cooked vegetables. Set aside and keep warm.
3. Place the fish fillets in a greased baking dish. Sprinkle with salt and pepper. Cover and cook in a 450°F (230°C) oven for 20 minutes, until the fish flakes easily with a fork.
4. Combine the Parmesan cheese and parsley. Top each fillet with 1 tbsp. (15 mL) grated Cheddar cheese, sprinkle with the Parmesan mixture and return to the oven, uncovered, for 5 minutes.
5. To serve, put about ¼ cup (60 mL) of the warm cream sauce on each plate and top with one of the fillets.

Serves 6.

* *Dymond Lake Seasoning*

Fish Cakes Suprême

These fish cakes, when teamed with our Mustard Dill Sauce from "Blueberries &
Polar Bears," give a whole new meaning to the term "Fish Burger". If it isn't a fish
burger that you are after, just serve them with the mustard sauce that follows,
Tomatoes Vinaigrette, page 118, Crispy Round Oven Fries, page 131, and dinner
is ready!

1 lb.	fresh boneless fillets of pike, pickerel or a similar firm white fish	500 g
¼ cup	finely chopped green onions	60 mL
¼ cup	mayonnaise	60 mL
1 cup	fresh bread crumbs soaked in milk; squeezed dry	250 mL
1	egg	1
1 tbsp.	chopped fresh parsley	15 mL
1 tbsp.	chopped fresh thyme OR 1 tsp. (5 mL) dried	15 mL
1 tbsp.	DLS* OR 1 tsp. (5 mL) salt and 2 tsp. (10 mL) pepper	15 mL
½ tsp.	salt	2 mL
½ cup	fresh bread crumbs	125 mL
½ cup	ground almonds	125 mL
3 tbsp.	vegetable oil	45 mL
3 tbsp.	butter OR margarine	45 mL

1. Cut the boneless fillets into thin strips and then into ¼" (6 mm) pieces. Place them in a bowl and add the onions, mayonnaise, soaked bread crumbs, egg, parsley, thyme, DLS* and salt.
2. Divide the mixture into 12 round patties.
3. Mix ½ cup (125 mL) of breadcrumbs and ground almonds. Dredge each patty in this mixture, patting to coat evenly with the crumbs.
4. Heat half the oil in a heavy frying pan and add half the butter. When it foams, add 6 of the fish cakes. Cover and cook over medium-high heat for 3 minutes per side. Drain on a wire rack in a warm spot. Add remaining oil and butter and cook the other 6 cakes.

Serves 4.

* Dymond Lake Seasoning

Creamy Mustard Sauce

¾ cup	heavy cream	175 mL
2 tbsp.	whole-grain mustard	30 mL

1. In a heavy saucepan, bring cream to a boil and simmer for 1 minute to thicken slightly. Remove from the heat and whisk in mustard.

Makes ¾ cup (175 mL) sauce.

  Moose, Goose & Things That Swim

WET YOUR WHISTLE

Ever try to whistle with a dry mouth? This section has absolutely nothing to do with whistling, but it does have some good remedies for "dry mouth"! Our most requested drink has been Pineapple Fruit Punch. (That's because we serve it at all our Book Launchings.) But there is something here for kids, special guests and large crowds, so go ahead – wet your whistle!

Banana Slush

Made with all fresh fruit, this takes a little more effort than most punches. It must be made up ahead of time and frozen until ready to serve.

5	bananas, mashed	5
5	oranges, juice of	5
5	lemons, juice of	5
4 cups	white sugar	1 L
7 cups	water	1.75 L
	ginger ale or similar soda	

1. Mix all together and freeze to make a slush. Serve half and half with ginger ale or a similar soda.

Makes about 4 quarts (4 L).

VARIATION: If you want a wine slush, add wine instead of soda to the slush when serving, or for a sparkling wine slush, add half wine and half soda water.

Frozen Fruit Shake

Ever wonder what to do with bananas that are past their prime? Peel them and store them in a sealable plastic bag in your freezer. Then reward your efforts with this fruit shake.

1	peeled, frozen banana	1
¼ cup	frozen strawberries, raspberries OR blueberries	60 mL
1 cup	orange juice	250 mL

1. Purée all together in a blender, and you have a slushy fruit drink with a terrific fresh fruit flavor.

Serves 1.

Goose Facts – When Do Geese Migrate??

The exact time of migration is impossible to predict with any accuracy. It is totally governed by seasons, but the geese have inside information about when winter or spring are REALLY going to arrive. At Dymond Lake Hunting Lodge, we estimate that the big migration south – when geese fly by the thousands, day and night – will come around the middle to the end of September. Before that, the geese cover smaller distances in every direction and stop to "feed" (themselves as well as the hunters!) The migration fills the skies for 2 or 3 days in any given area.

  Wet Your Whistle

Orange Julius

With or without the egg, you can dress up your morning orange juice for a special occasion.

6 oz.	can frozen orange juice concentrate	178 mL
1 cup	milk	250 mL
1 cup	water	250 mL
¼ cup	white sugar	60 mL
1 tsp.	vanilla	5 mL
2	eggs (optional)	2
10-12	ice cubes	10-12

1. Put all together in a blender and process until ice is finely crushed. Serve immediately.

Yields 6 cups (1.5 L).

See photograph on page 69.

Pineapple Fruit Punch

This punch recipe is requested wherever we use it. It is embarrassingly simple and consistently delicious.

12 oz.	can frozen orange juice concentrate	355 mL
12 oz.	can frozen lemonade concentrate	355 mL
4 cups	pineapple juice*	1 L
2 qt.	bottle ginger ale or similar soda	2 L

1. Mix juices together, smoothing out the lumps of the concentrates. Add soda and serve. Garnish with orange slices. Add ice, if desired.

Makes 4 quarts (4 L).

* *or a large can of juice – size isn't very important.*

VARIATION: For a Pineapple Wine Punch, use a 32 oz. (1 L) bottle of white wine and a 32 oz. (1 L) bottle of 7-up instead of the ginger ale.

Moses wouldn't have had to wander in the wilderness for forty years if he had stopped to ask directions.

Pink Pastel Punch

A special occasion punch that gives you something to chew on!

1 qt.	raspberry sherbet	1 L
12 oz.	can frozen pink lemonade	355 mL
4 cups	cold water	1 L
1 qt.	bottle ginger ale or similar soda, chilled	1 L
2 x 10 oz.	pkg. frozen raspberries, thawed	2 x 283 g

1. Mix all together, adding raspberries last. Serve immediately.

Makes 4 quarts (4 L).

VARIATION: This is delicious with strawberry sherbet and frozen strawberries.

Tea Essence

When serving tea to a crowd, it is worth making up some essence ahead of time. This eliminates the brewing time. Just add water and the tea is ready to serve.

1¼ cups	tea leaves	300 mL
5 cups	boiling water	1.25 L

1. Combine and let steep in a bowl for 10 minutes, then strain. Keep essence in the refrigerator until ready to use. Keeps for 6 weeks.
2. To use, add ⅔ cup (150 mL) essence to an 8-cup (2 L) teapot. Fill with boiling water and serve immediately.

Makes 4 cups (1 L) of essence; 70 teacups.

Crab Apple Liqueur

We had a lot of fun experimenting with this one! Conclusion? You can't go wrong, so why not make it as quick and simple as possible!

1 gallon	crab apples	4 L
4 cups	white sugar	1 L
26 oz.	vodka	750 mL
4	1-quart jars with tight fitting lids OR a 1-gallon (4 L) jar	4

  *Wet Your Whistle*

Crab Apple Liqueur

Continued

1. Wash crab apples, and remove stems and flower ends. (It made no difference to the liqueur whether apples were cut, scored, or not.
2. Pack apples into 4 quart-sized jars or 1 gallon (4 L) jar.
3. Pour sugar over apples – 1 cup (250 mL) per quart (1 L), or all into the gallon (4 L) jar. Shake the sugar down into the jar(s).
4. Add vodka – ¾ cup (175 mL) per quart (1 L), or all into the gallon jar.
5. Let sit 24 hours, then shake gently to help sugar to dissolve. Turn upside down and let sit for 24 hours. Repeat the turning for 14 days.
5. On the 15th day, strain the liqueur through several layers of cheesecloth, and bottle.

Makes 2 quarts (2 L) of liqueur.

VARIATION: For a slightly stronger tasting liqueur, use only ½ cup (125 mL) sugar and ½ cup (125 mL) vodka per quart (1 L) of apples.

"I'm Not A Bear"

(Helen) It was late in August and Doug and I were at Dymond Lake along with a few friends, getting things ready for hunting season. We had just finished our main course and were ready for dessert. This was still back in the days before we had electricity or any type of refrigeration, so I had to go outside to get the whipping cream out of a cooler. It was dark and it was also POLAR BEAR SEASON. On my way out the door, I turned and said "If I scream you'll know there is a bear out here." Well, I stepped out the door, heard something, automatically screamed and backed into the cabin. The next thing I heard was four shells being loaded into four shotguns – and at the same time a voice outside yelling "I'm not a bear, I'm not a bear." We were in the middle of nowhere and unexpected visitors normally arrived by helicopter or airplane – and you could hear those coming! Who had managed to sneak up on the camp? George Hicks, a friend from Churchill, and an Inuit couple from Arviat, N.W.T., had taken a speed boat from Arviat to Churchill along the shore of Hudson Bay. The motor had quit just before they got to the mouth of the Churchill River, and they had drifted helplessly on Hudson Bay for five hours before being blown to a spot where they could get to shore. This was quite remarkable in that if the wind had been blowing out into the Bay, they probably would never have been found! They hit shore about three miles north of our cabin at Dymond Lake and George knew there was a very good chance we would be there and would deliver them to Churchill.

We found them beds for the night and woke up the next morning to "SOLID FOG". You could not see two feet in front of you. George knew that they were going to be worried about him in Churchill because he had been expected the day before and now he was going to be two days late. We watched the weather all day and finally at high tide that night, we went down to our boat to look the situation over. We were seriously considering heading out in the fog. Thank goodness our friend, Ernie, finally said, "I'm not going anywhere in this mess." That was enough for the rest of us to come to our senses. We woke up the next day to sunshine and good winds!

Eggnog

Comparatively speaking, here is a light and easy recipe for holiday entertaining. The amount of liquor added is a personal preference and, in fact, is optional.

12	eggs	12
1½ cups	icing sugar	375 mL
½ tsp.	salt	2 mL
4 tbsp.	vanilla	60 mL
10 cups	whole milk	2.5 L
½ cup	brandy, rum, rye or sherry (or more)	125 mL
2 cups	whipping cream	500 mL
¼ cup	icing sugar	60 mL
	nutmeg	

1. Beat eggs well. Add sugar, salt and vanilla and continue to beat. Blend in milk and liquor. Refrigerate for 24 hours.
2. Pour the eggnog into a punch bowl. Whip the cream with the icing sugar and spoon it over the eggnog. Sprinkle with nutmeg.

Makes about 4 quarts (4 L) of eggnog.

Moose Milk

The drink that you eat – definitely not for kids!

13 oz.	dark rum	375 mL
8 oz.	Kahlúa	250 mL
1 qt.	milk	1 L
2 qts.	vanilla ice cream	2 L
	cinnamon	
	nutmeg	

1. Mix the rum, Kahlúa and milk in a punch bowl. Add the ice cream by the scoop. Let it melt a little, stir, then sprinkle with cinnamon and nutmeg. Add ice cubes – it won't hurt to dilute this a little!

Makes about 2½ quarts (2.5 L).

*Inuit man to his bride, "Just think, Honey, our own little igloo.
Then, maybe some day, the chatter of little teeth!"*

Wet Your Whistle

Bread & Breakfast

Yeast breads are a real specialty for both Marie and me. We are usually the ones called on to make the buns for potlucks or special events. Gary, Marie's husband, says it's a little disconcerting, sometimes, when one of his parishioners walks up to him and says, "I sure like your wife's buns!"

We want to share with you some of our more traditional family recipes – things that have been shared for years with our friends and enjoyed by our extended families. So, from Helen we get Christmas Danish; while from Marie we have Christmas Bread and Hot Cross Buns. In keeping with our northern experience, we have included some sourdough recipes. And, of course, many more breakfasts, muffins and breads.

Baking With Yeast

Most, though not all, of the recipes in this section use yeast. Therefore, we would like to share some of the things we have learned, through experience, about baking with yeast. This is so important it is repeated from our first book "Blueberries & Polar Bears".

Water Temperature: When using tap water in a bread recipe, the water should feel quite warm when tested on the inside of your wrist, but not hot! For experienced bread makers this will sound very elementary, but the rest of you can learn from two who learned to make bread by trial and error on their own — it is important to the success of the product. Hot water destroys yeast.

Rising Techniques: When setting the dough in a warm place to rise, cover it with a cloth or tea towel. Helen also puts a piece of plastic over the dry cloth. She finds that it keeps the top of the dough from drying out and creates more warmth in the dough. Marie doesn't bother with it and her results are just as good so go with whichever method you prefer.

For Evenly Baked Breads: When using 2 racks of your oven at the same time, switch the pans from top to bottom, and visa versa, halfway through the baking time.

Oven Temperature: Always use a preheated oven.

Oil vs. Butter or Margarine: When making bread & buns, we use oil instead of butter or margarine. We do this for convenience and find that it works just as well.

Quality of Flour: Over the years, we have tried many kinds of flour. We have found no difference in the taste and quality of our breads, whether we used a name brand or a no-name brand. Occasionally, there was a slight difference in the degree of whiteness.

Types of Yeast: Our recipes are all written for the use of INSTANT YEAST, but quick-rising yeast works just as well. For QUICK-RISING YEAST, take 1 cup (250 mL) of the water called for in the recipe, and put it in a small bowl with 1 tsp. (5 mL) sugar. Sprinkle the yeast over the water, letting it fall from a distance of at least 6" (15 cm). This forces the yeast to go beneath the surface of the water where it dissolves more easily. Do not stir. Put in a warm place to sit until yeast mixture has become bubbly, about 5 minutes. Add to recipe as directed.

Freezing and Thawing Tips: Break buns apart and slice bread before freezing. This way, you thaw only what you want to use immediately. Frozen slices of bread can be toasted without thawing first. To thaw a frozen loaf of bread, put it in the microwave, uncovered, on high heat for 2 minutes. 1 bun takes 30 seconds.

Greasing Pans or Working Surfaces: When the recipe calls for greased pans or surfaces, we use a nonstick cooking spray that is environmentally safe.

Shaping Buns: Spread your fingers, palm side down, into the shape of a spider; place your curved fingers over the dough and move your hand in circular motions on the greased surface, putting a little pressure on the dough. With practice, you will quickly shape the dough into a smooth ball. With more practice, you will be doing it with both hands at once!

Whole-Wheat Bagels

Bagels seem to be the "in thing"! So, here is a very health-conscious variety – lots of fiber and great taste.

2 cups	warm water	500 mL
2 tbsp.	honey	30 mL
1 tbsp.	salt	15 mL
2½ cups	whole-wheat flour	625 mL
2 tbsp.	instant yeast*	30 mL
2½ cups	white flour	625 mL
	cornmeal	
1	egg white, beaten	1
1 tbsp.	cold water	15 mL
	sesame seeds OR rolled oats (optional)	

1. Combine water, honey and salt. Add the whole-wheat flour and the yeast. Beat for 2 minutes, using an electric mixer or a whisk.
2. Switch to a dough hook and work in enough of the white flour to make a soft dough OR, by hand, turn the dough onto a well-floured surface and knead until smooth and elastic, 8-10 minutes.
3. Place the dough in an ungreased bowl, cover with a cloth and let rise for 45 minutes. It will not double in bulk.
4. Punch down the dough and turn it onto a lightly floured surface. Divide the dough into 12 equal pieces; roll each piece into a smooth ball. Poke your finger through the center of the ball and twirl or shape dough into a doughnut shape with a large hole. Place on a lightly floured surface, cover and let rise for 30 minutes.
5. Bring 1¾" (4 cm) water to a gentle boil in a large pan. (We use a large roaster.) If the hole in the bagel has closed up at this point, gently stretch the bagel out then lower the bagel into the boiling water. You may boil several at one time but don't crowd them. Simmer them for 5 minutes, turning 3 times per side.
6. Remove the bagels from the water and place them on a towel to cool for 5 minutes. Place them on a greased baking sheet which has been sprinkled lightly with cornmeal.
7. Brush the bagels with the combined egg white and cold water and sprinkle them with sesame seeds or rolled oats, if desired. Bake at 400°F (200°C) for 30 minutes, or until nicely browned
8. Remove the bagels from the pan and cool them on a wire rack.

Makes 12 giant bagels.

* *See Yeast, Rising Techniques, Shaping Buns and Freezing Tips, page 50.*

VARIATION: CINNAMON AND RAISIN BAGELS – Proceed as above and add an extra tbsp. (15 mL) of sugar, 1 tsp. (5 mL) of cinnamon, ½ tsp. (2 mL) cloves and ¾ cup (175 mL) of raisins to the dough. Also add 1 tbsp. (15 mL) honey or sugar to the boiling water.

Sourdough Starter

(HELEN) This recipe came to us through Sandy Sims, a friend of Marie's since her early married days in Big Trout Lake. They also ended up living in Churchill at the same time in 1976 and of course that is where I met Sandy. Sandy is a nurse by profession and, this past fall, Marie managed to convince her that she should take a break and come help out at Dymond Lake. Some break, having to get up at 4 o'clock every morning! We picked up some great new recipes from her and have forgiven her for calling us "Fanatical Berry Pickers" just because we go out in any spare minute we have, no matter what the weather!

Sourdough Starter or Sponge

2 cups	flour	500 mL
2 cups	warm water	500 mL
1 tbsp.	instant yeast*	15 mL
½ cup	sugar	125 mL

1. Combine all ingredients in a 2-quart (2 L) glass or plastic container and place in a warm place overnight. In the morning it should be bubbly and frothy. It is now called a sponge. For each cup (250 mL) of starter you use in a recipe, you must add 1 cup (250 mL) of flour, 1 cup (250 mL) of milk and ¼ cup (60 mL) of white sugar to the original mixture before returning it to the refrigerator. Place starter in a sterile jar or container with a tight lid. Refrigerate for future use.

Sourdough Biscuits

1 cup	flour	250 mL
½ tsp.	baking soda	2 mL
2 tsp.	baking powder	10 mL
½ tsp.	salt	2 mL
1 cup	sourdough starter	250 mL
⅓ cup	oil	75 mL

1. Stir together flour, baking soda, baking powder and salt.
2. Add the sourdough starter and oil. Stir just until moistened.
3. Turn out onto lightly floured board and pat out to ¾" (2 cm) thickness. Cut with a 2" (5 cm) round cutter.
4. Place on a greased baking pan and bake at 400°F (200°C) for 12-15 minutes.

Makes 12 small biscuits.

VARIATION: You can add grated cheese, raisins or currants to the dough.

Bread & Breakfast

Sourdough Pancakes

3	eggs, beaten	3
1 cup	milk	250 mL
2 cups	sourdough starter	500 mL
1¾ cups	flour	425 mL
2 tsp.	baking soda	10 mL
2 tsp.	salt	10 mL
¼ cup	white sugar	60 mL
¼ cup	melted butter OR margarine	60 mL

1. Beat together eggs, milk, starter, flour, baking soda, salt, sugar and melted butter.
2. Cook on a hot, oiled griddle until lightly browned on one side. Flip pancake and brown on other side.

Makes 10 large or 20 small pancakes.

SERVING SUGGESTION: Serve with butter and Pancake Syrup, page 201, OR brown sugar and lemon OR cinnamon, OR fruit preserves and whipped cream.

Sourdough Bread

2 cups	sourdough starter	500 mL
2 tbsp.	vegetable oil	30 mL
1 tsp.	salt	5 mL
2-3 cups	flour	500-750 mL
1 tbsp.	yeast	15 mL

1. Take out 2 cups (500 mL) of starter and put in a medium bowl. Cover and leave in a warm place overnight. (OR microwave for 90 seconds until warm and bubbly – it's a new era!)
2. Add oil, salt and 1 cup (250 mL) of flour to the starter; beat well with a wooden spoon. Continue to add flour until you have a soft dough.
3. Turn out on a floured board and knead for 8 minutes.
4. Place in a greased 5 x 9" (13 x 23 cm) bread pan, cover and put in a warm place to rise until almost double, 2½ hours. We have found that it rises more when you put it in the oven to bake.
5. Bake at 350°F (190°C) for 30 minutes.

Makes 1 loaf.

NOTE: Traditional sourdough bread is firmer and heavier than yeast bread – not quite what we are used to. The addition of yeast maintains the flavor and immensely improves the texture. Sometimes it's okay to cheat!.

Pizza Bread

Make Bread Sticks from this dough, or small loaves to eat with a meal. Or, use it for an excellent taste teaser, Pizza Bread with Cheese, page 57.

1½ cups	spaghetti sauce	375 mL
½ cup	hot water	125 mL
1 tbsp.	sugar	15 mL
1 tsp.	salt	5 mL
3 tbsp.	vegetable oil	45 mL
¼ cup	finely chopped jalapeño peppers	60 mL
2	garlic cloves, minced	2
2 tsp.	dried oregano, OR 2 tbsp. (30 mL) chopped fresh	10 mL
2 tsp.	dried basil, OR 2 tbsp. (30 mL) chopped fresh	10 mL
4½ cups	flour (approximately)	1.125 L
1 tbsp.	instant yeast*	15 mL
	butter OR margarine	
	garlic salt	

1. In a large bowl, combine spaghetti sauce, water, sugar, salt, oil, jalapeños, garlic, oregano and basil. This mixture will have to be warmed a little if the hot water did not do the trick. Add 2 cups (500 mL) flour and the yeast*. Mix well with an electric mixer or a wire whisk.
2. Gradually add remaining flour and work into the dough either with the dough hook on your mixer or by hand. If by hand, turn dough out onto a well-floured surface and work flour into dough with a kneading motion, until dough feels soft and velvety, 8-10 minutes. You may need MORE or LESS flour.
3. Shape dough into a ball, place in a well-greased bowl, turning dough to grease the surface. Cover, put in a warm place and let rise until doubled in size, about an hour.
4. Punch down dough and shape as desired:

Pizza Bread Sticks

Divide dough into 64 pieces. Roll each on a greased surface, using flat hands and rolling the dough into a stick with a ½" (1.3 cm) diameter. Length will vary. To bake see page 57.
Makes 64 breadsticks.

Pizza Taste Teaser Sticks

Divide dough into 8 pieces. On a greased surface, shape dough into long, thin loaves 1" (2.5 cm) in diameter. Length will vary. To bake see page 57.
Makes 8 sticks.

  Bread & Breakfast

Pizza Bread Loaves

Divide dough in half and, on a greased surface, shape each half into a loaf using a kneading motion, or use a rolling pin to roll out the dough and then roll it into a loaf.

Makes 2 loaves.

5. Place the sticks (loaves) on (in) a well-greased baking sheet (5 x 9" [13 x 23 cm] bread pan), cover and let rise for 1 hour, or until doubled in size.
6. Uncover and bake at 350°F (180°C) Bread Sticks for 15 minutes; Taste Teaser Sticks for 20 minutes; loaves for 25 minutes.
7. Remove from trays (pans) to a cooling rack.
8. Immediately brush BREAD STICKS with butter or margarine and sprinkle with garlic salt. Do the same with the other variations, if desired.

SERVING SUGGESTIONS: Slice loaves of bread, butter them on both sides, sprinkle with garlic salt and fry on both sides.

TASTE TEASER STICKS may be cut in chunks and eaten as buns OR use in the following hors d'oeuvre.

* See note on YEAST on page 50.

Pizza Bread with Cheese

Make the pizza bread recipe on the previous page into Taste Teaser Sticks.

pizza bread
grated mozzarella cheese

1. Slice the Taste Teaser Sticks in ¼" (6 mm) slices. Place on a greased baking sheet.
2. Sprinkle mozzarella over each slice.
3. Bake at 350°F (180°C) until cheese is melted. Serve hot.

See photograph on page 121.

Max and Moe were out fishing and were catching a fish on every cast. Said Max, "We'll have to remember this place somehow so we can come back." " Great!" said Moe. "All we have to do is mark an X on the bottom of the boat." "Yeah right, stupid!" said Max, "How do you know that we're going to get the same boat?"

Herbed Focaccia

Here is a recipe for the 90s. Herbed bread wasn't even in our repertoire in the 80s but we certainly enjoy it now. In fact, we are working on a spacious greenhouse at North Knife so we can grow fresh herbs during the season.

1 cup	warm water	205 mL
1 tsp.	white sugar	5 mL
1 tbsp.	instant yeast*	15 mL
2½ cups	white flour	625 mL
2 tbsp.	olive oil	30 mL
1 tsp.	salt	5 mL
½ tsp.	EACH dried sage, rosemary and marjoram, OR	2 mL
	1½ tsp. (7 mL) EACH of chopped fresh	
2 tbsp.	cornmeal	30 mL

Onion Rosemary Topping:

3 tbsp.	olive oil	45 mL
1	onion, thinly sliced (approx. 1 cup [250 mL])	1
½ tsp.	dried rosemary	2 mL

1. In a medium-sized bowl, combine water, sugar, yeast and 1 cup (250 mL) of flour. Beat for 2 minutes with an electric mixer. Cover lightly with a cloth* and let stand for 30 minutes.
2. Stir in olive oil, salt, sage, rosemary, marjoram and enough of the flour to make a smooth, soft dough. Use your dough hook if you have one. If not, turn out on a floured surface and knead in enough flour to make a soft dough. Knead about 5 minutes.
3. Place dough in a greased bowl, turning it over to grease the top. Cover with a towel and let rise in a warm place for 1 hour, or until doubled in bulk.
4. Gently punch down dough; turn it out onto a lightly floured surface. Divide dough in half, cover with a cloth and let it rest for 5 minutes.
5. Roll out each half into an 8" (20 cm) circle. Sprinkle cornmeal over the baking sheets. Place dough circles on trays; cover them with a cloth and let them rise for 30 minutes, or until doubled in size.
6. Heat oil over medium-low heat. Add onion and rosemary and cook for 7-10 minutes, until onions are soft and golden. Let cool.
7. When dough has risen, press your fingers into it, almost to the bottom, to make dimples. Spread onion mixture over loaves. Bake at 400°F (200°C) for 20-25 minutes, until golden and hollow sounding when lightly tapped.

Makes 2.

* *See notes on Yeast on page 50.*

Bread & Breakfast

Oatmeal Molasses Bread

(HELEN) My daughter, Jeannie, produced this recipe at North Knife last summer and it soon became a favorite. We discovered that it was great rolled into little round loaves and thinly cut for hors d'oeuvres. We spread the bread with a thin layer of cream cheese, and added a slice of smoked fish, capers and chopped red onion. It was wonderful. We also found it made great melba toast. As well as all that it was delicious by itself, for sandwiches and for toast.

1¾ cups	boiling water	425 mL
1 cup	rolled oats	250 mL
6 tbsp.	molasses OR more, if you like	90 mL
⅓ cup	oil	75 mL
1 tsp.	salt	5 mL
5-6 cups	flour	1.25-1.5 L
2 tbsp.	instant yeast*	30 mL
2	eggs, beaten	2

1. In a large bowl, combine the boiling water, rolled oats, molasses, oil and salt. Cool to lukewarm.
2. With an electric mixer or wire whisk, beat in 2 cups (500 mL) of the flour, the yeast and the beaten eggs.
3. Gradually add the remaining flour and work it into the dough, either with a dough hook on the mixer or by hand. If by hand, turn the dough out onto a well-floured surface and work in the flour with a kneading motion, until the dough feels soft, smooth and velvety, 8-10 minutes. You may need MORE or LESS flour.
4. Shape the dough into a ball and place it in a large, well-greased bowl, turning dough to grease the surface. Cover the bowl with a cloth and put it in a warm place to rise until doubled in size, about 1 hour.
5. Punch down the dough and turn it out onto a well-greased surface. For regular loaves, cut the dough in 2, shape it into loaves and place the loaves in 2 well-greased 5 x 9" (13 x 23 cm) loaf pans. For hors d'oeuvre loaves, divide the dough into 6 equal pieces and shape them into long, thin loaves, like a small French stick.
6. Cover and let rise until doubled, 45-60 minutes.
7. Bake loaves at 375°F (190°C) for 30-40 minutes for regular size; 20 minutes for small loaves.

Makes 2 regular loaves OR 6 hors d'oeuvre sticks.

VARIATION: To make melba toast, slice an hors d'oeuvre loaf thinly and bake at 325°F (160°C) until crispy, 20-30 minutes.

* *See Yeast, Rising Techniques, Shaping Buns and Freezing Tips, on page 50.*

Crunchy Brown Buns

These delicious buns were a result of Marie's quest for a flavorful, crunchy, whole-grain bun. We use Red River Cereal which is a combination of cracked wheat, rye and flax – but a similar whole-grain cereal would do.

2½ cups	warm water	625 mL
¼ cup	oil	60 mL
2 tbsp.	sugar	30 mL
2 tsp.	salt	10 mL
1	egg	1
½ cup	Red River cereal (uncooked)	125 mL
¼ cup	cornmeal	60 mL
1 cup	oatmeal	250 mL
¼ cup	sunflower seeds	60 mL
1 cup	whole-wheat flour	250 mL
4 cups	white flour	1 L
2 tbsp.	instant yeast*	30 mL
1	egg white	1
	oatmeal	

1. In a large mixing bowl, combine water, oil, sugar, salt, egg, cereal, cornmeal, oatmeal, sunflower seeds, whole-wheat flour, 2 cups (500 mL) white flour and yeast. Mix with an electric mixer or whisk.
2. Gradually add the remaining flour and work it into the dough, either with a dough hook on the mixer, or by hand. If by hand, turn the dough out onto a well-floured surface and work in the flour with a kneading motion, until the dough feels soft, smooth and velvety, 8-10 minutes. You may need MORE or LESS flour.
3. Place the dough in a well-greased bowl, turning the dough to grease the top. Cover the dough with a cloth and put it in a warm place to rise until doubled in size, about an hour.
4. Punch down the dough and turn it out onto a well-greased surface. With a bread knife, cut the dough into 2 equal pieces. Cut each ½ into 12 equal pieces and shape them into buns. Place them on a greased tray, cover with a cloth* and put them in a warm place to rise until doubled, about an hour.
5. Brush top of buns with beaten egg white and sprinkle with oatmeal.
6. Bake at 400°F (200°C) for 15 minutes. Remove the buns from the pans and cool them on cooling racks.

Makes 2 dozen buns.

* *See Yeast, Rising Techniques, Shaping Buns and Freezing Tips, page 50.*

See photograph on page 87.

Hot Cross Buns

(MARIE) It is a tradition in our family to make Hot Cross Buns every Lenten season. They take longer than regular buns, but don't try any shortcuts or you'll shortchange yourself.

2½ cups	milk	625 mL
2 tbsp.	white sugar	30 mL
7 cups	flour (approx.)	1.75 L
2 tbsp.	instant yeast*	30 mL
½ cup	butter OR margarine, melted	125 mL
1 cup	white sugar	250 mL
2	eggs	2
1 tsp.	salt	5 mL
1 tsp.	cinnamon	5 mL
½ tsp.	cloves	2 mL
½ cup	grated orange peel**(about 2 oranges)	125 mL
1 cup	raisins	250 mL

1. Heat the milk just until lukewarm.
2. Add the 2 tbsp. (30 mL) sugar, 3 cups (750 mL) of the flour and the yeast. Beat well with an electric mixer.
3. Cover and let rise for 45 minutes.
4. In a separate bowl, combine all the remaining ingredients except the remaining flour. Add this mixture to the yeast mixture.
5. Switch to a dough hook, if you have one, and add the remaining 4 cups (1 L) of flour, gradually. Knead it until dough isn't too sticky to handle. If kneading by hand, add as much flour as you can in the bowl, then turn out onto a floured surface, and work in the rest of the flour by hand, using a kneading motion. It may take a little MORE or a little LESS flour. Just knead the dough until it feels soft but not sticky, and bounces back when pressed, 8-10 minutes.
6. Shape dough into a ball; place in a large, well-greased bowl, turning dough to grease surface. Cover it with a cloth*, put it in a warm place and let rise until doubled in size, an hour or longer.
7. Punch down dough. Divide in half and let rest for 10 minutes.
8. Shape each half into 18 buns*. Place buns 1" (2.5 cm) apart on a well-greased baking sheet or pan. Cover and let rise at least 1 hour in a warm place.
9. Bake in a preheated 375°F (190°C) oven for 13-15 minutes.

Makes 3 dozen buns.

* *See notes on Yeast, Rising Techniques and Shaping Buns on page 50.*

** *I like to use freshly grated orange peel, but dried, candied peel may be substituted or use half of each.*

Christmas Danish

This flaky pastry is so good, it mightn't make it to Christmas. A lovely breakfast or dessert Danish, it is appropriate anytime. BUT before you start, check your calendar. It takes 3 days to complete this recipe!

½ cup	milk	125 mL
¼ cup	butter OR margarine	60 mL
1 cup	warm water	250 mL
½ cup	white sugar	125 mL
1½ tsp.	salt	7 mL
¼ cup	cornstarch	60 mL
1½ tsp.	dried grated lemon peel OR 3 tsp. (15 mL) fresh	7 mL
2	eggs, separated	2
3½ cups	flour (approx.)	825 mL
2 tbsp.	instant yeast*	30 mL
1½ cups	butter OR margarine, room temperature	375 mL
1 tbsp.	water	15 mL

DAY 1

1. Combine milk and butter in a saucepan. Heat just until butter melts. Remove from heat and pour into a large bowl. Add the lukewarm water, sugar, salt, cornstarch and lemon peel.
2. Add 2 egg yolks, 1 egg white (reserve other egg white), 1½ cups (375 mL) flour and yeast. Beat until smooth.
3. Stir in an additional 1¾ cups (425 mL) flour to make a stiff batter. You may need MORE or LESS flour. Stir just until blended.
4. Cover tightly with a lid or aluminum foil. Chill for about an hour.
5. On waxed paper, spread 1½ cups (375 mL) butter into a 10 x 12" (25 x 30 cm) rectangle. Cover with plastic wrap, then chill for 1 hour.
6. On a lightly floured surface, roll the chilled dough into a 12 x 16" (30 x 40 cm) rectangle.
7. Place butter slab on ⅔ of the dough. Fold the uncovered third over the middle section; cover with the remaining third. Give the dough a quarter turn; roll it into a 12 x 16" (30 x 40 cm) rectangle; fold as above. Turn, roll and fold once more. Cover with plastic wrap, then chill for 1 hour.
8. Repeat procedure of 2 rollings, foldings, turnings and chillings 2 more times. Refrigerate dough overnight.

DAY 2

9. On a lightly floured surface, divide dough in half. Roll ½ the dough into a 6 x 15" (15 x 38 cm) rectangle**. Cut 12 strips, ½" (1.25 cm) wide x 15" (38 cm) long. Twist each strip and then roll it into a circle like a snail, sealing the ends well.
10. Place Danish pastries on greased baking sheets. Cover tightly with plastic wrap. Refrigerate pastries overnight.

Bread & Breakfast

DAY 3

11. Combine reserved egg white with 1 tbsp. (15 mL) water. Brush on rolls.
12. Bake pastries at 375°F (190°C) about 15-20 minutes, or until done. (Finally!)
13. Remove from baking sheets and cool on wire racks. When cool, drizzle with the following icing, and decorate with colored sprinkles or sliced almonds, if desired.

VARIATION: If you wish, put a small spoonful of cream cheese or lemon curd or apricot preserves in the center of the pastry before drizzling with icing.

Vanilla Icing

1 cup	sifted icing sugar	250 mL
¼ tsp.	vanilla	1 mL
1 tbsp.	milk (approx.)	15 mL

Combine icing sugar and vanilla with enough milk to make a soft icing.

Makes 24 pastries.

NOTE: If timing is a problem you can wait LONGER to perform each step, but don't give it less time.

* *See note on YEAST on page 50.*
** *As an alternative shape, roll dough into a circle. Cut into 12 wedges, like a pie. Roll each wedge from the wide end, then bend to form a croissant.*

Wait For Me – I'm The Pilot!

Those of you who are pilots will know that airplanes, like most machines, have their little idiosyncrasies. One of our planes just would not start after it was turned off, until the engine had cooled down. We had the mechanics check it over a number of times but they could not find the problem, so Doug just had to live with it that summer. It was rather inconvenient, though, if he had to fly into one of the outcamps to drop something off, especially if there was no one to help him dock. He got quite proficient at beaching the plane at Small Lake, tying it to a tree and just letting it idle while he unloaded. One afternoon, he arrived in my kitchen at North Knife dripping wet and looking a little sheepish. I, of course, thought he had fallen off the dock at North Knife Lake but when I questioned him, a different story emerged. Apparently, he had landed at Small Lake, beached the airplane successfully and tied it securely (he thought) to a tree. He unloaded the plane and was busy doing something when he turned to see the airplane starting to putt, putt away. He went tearing after it and just managed to grab onto the rope. There he was, all by himself, being dragged through the water by his plane. He managed to pull himself hand over hand on the rope until he reached the float, climbed on and got into the airplane before it ran into the far shore. I was sorry that no one had been around to video the scene, I am sure it would have been a winner for "America's Funniest".

Christmas Bread

(MARIE) A Christmas tradition in the Woolsey house. Every year I wonder why we don't eat it all year long. This is very good for gift-giving!

2½ cups	lukewarm water	625 mL
½ cup	white sugar	125 mL
1 tsp.	salt	5 mL
¼ cup	vegetable oil	60 mL
1	egg	1
2 tsp.	ground cardamom OR anise	10 mL
1 cup	raisins	250 mL
½ cup	candied peel	125 mL
½ cup	candied cherries, halved	125 mL
6 cups	flour (approx.)	1.5 L
2 tbsp.	instant yeast*	30 mL
1	egg white	1
1 tbsp.	water	250 mL

1. In a large mixing bowl, combine water, sugar, salt, oil, egg, cardamom, raisins, peel and cherries. Add 3 cups (750 mL) of flour and the yeast. Beat well.
2. Switch to a dough hook, if you have one, and add the remaining 3 cups (750 mL) of flour, gradually. Knead until dough isn't too sticky to handle. If kneading by hand, add as much flour as you can in the bowl, then turn out onto a floured surface, and work in the rest of the flour by hand, using a kneading motion. It may take a little MORE or a little LESS flour. Just knead it until the dough feels soft but not sticky, and bounces back when pressed, 8-10 minutes.
3. Shape dough into a ball, and place it in a large, well-greased bowl, turning dough to grease surface. Cover the dough with a cloth* and put it in a warm place to rise, until doubled in size, about an hour.
4. Punch down dough and cut it into 3 or 4 pieces. Form each piece into a round loaf. Place the loaves on greased cookie sheets, 2 loaves to a sheet; cover and let rise in a warm place until doubled in size.
5. Brush with egg white and water. Bake at 350°F (180°C) for 30 minutes.
6. Remove baked loaves from baking sheets and let cool on a rack.

Makes 3 large or 4 small round loaves.

COOKING TIP: Cardamom is a unique and wonderful spice with a warm, sweet, spicy flavor. Anise gives a mild flavor of black licorice. I can't decide which I like better. Don't be afraid to add a little extra spice for a more pronounced flavor.

* *See notes on Yeast and Rising Tips on page 50.*

Cranberry Go Round

This was a Christmas favorite for my sister, Louise, (Gavin's wife) back in the days when she spent time in the kitchen. Now he does the cooking!

1 cup	milk	250 mL
½ cup	butter OR margarine	125 mL
½ cup	warm water	125 mL
½ cup	sugar	125 mL
1 tsp.	salt	5 mL
1	egg, beaten	1
3-4 cups	flour	750 mL-1 L
1 tbsp.	instant yeast	15 mL
½ cup	flour	125 mL
½ cup	firmly packed brown sugar	125 mL
½ cup	chopped pecans	125 mL
1½ cups	cranberries, fresh OR frozen	375 mL

Vanilla Frosting:

1 cup	icing sugar	250 mL
½ tsp.	vanilla	2 mL
	milk	

1. Heat milk and butter until quite warm but not hot.
2. Pour into a large bowl and add water, sugar, salt, egg, 2 cups (500 mL) of flour and the yeast. Beat well with an electric mixer or whisk.
3. Gradually add enough of the remaining flour to make a stiff batter. Note that it is a stiff batter, not a dough. Use your dough hook if you have one, if not mix flour in by hand.
4. Cover the bowl tightly with aluminum foil and refrigerate for at least 2 hours. (The dough may be kept in the refrigerator for up to 3 days.)
5. When ready to shape, combine flour, brown sugar and pecans.
6. Turn the dough onto a lightly floured board and divide it in half. Roll one half into a 7 x 14" (18 x 35 cm) rectangle. Spread with ¾ cup (175 mL) of cranberries, then sprinkle with ½ of the brown sugar mixture. Roll it up from the long side as for a jelly roll. Seal the long edge. Form the roll into a circle and place it, sealed side down, on a greased baking sheet. Seal the ends together firmly. Cut slits ⅔ of the way through the ring at 1" (2.5 cm) intervals; turn each circle on its side, so that it overlaps the one beside it. Repeat with the remaining dough on another cookie sheet.
7. Cover and let rise in a warm place until double, for 1-2 hours. (This will depend on how long the dough has chilled.)
8. Bake at 375°F (190°C) for 20-25 minutes.
9. Combine frosting ingredients, using just enough milk to make a drizzly icing. Frost warm cake on a wire rack.

Makes 2 rings.

Bread & Breakfast 65

Cranberry Streusel Coffee Cake

A lovely cranberry-laced coffee cake that looks as good as it tastes. Great for a brunch, coffee party or with a dollop of whipped cream for dessert.

Cinnamon Streusel:

¾ cup	brown sugar	175 mL
½ cup	flour	125 mL
1 tsp.	cinnamon	5 mL
¼ cup	butter OR margarine	60 mL

Cranberry Coffee Cake:

½ cup	butter OR margarine, softened	125 mL
1 cup	white sugar	250 mL
2	eggs	2
2 cups	flour	500 mL
1 tsp.	baking powder	5 mL
1 tsp.	baking soda	5 mL
½ tsp.	salt	2 mL
1 tbsp.	lemon juice OR vinegar	15 mL
1 cup	whipping cream OR evaporated milk	250 mL
2 cups	cranberries, fresh OR frozen	500 mL

1. Mix together streusel ingredients until crumbly. Set aside.
2. With an electric mixer, in a large bowl, cream butter and sugar. Add eggs and beat well.
3. In a smaller bowl, mix flour, baking powder, baking soda and salt.
4. In a measuring cup, add lemon juice to cream and mix to make it sour.
5. Add dry ingredients to butter mixture, alternately with soured cream, beating well after each addition.
6. Spread ½ of batter in a greased and floured 10" (25 cm) springform pan, bundt pan or angel food pan. Sprinkle 1 cup (250 mL) cranberries and ½ of streusel mixture over batter. Spread with remaining batter. Sprinkle evenly with remaining cranberries. Press cranberries lightly into batter. Sprinkle with remaining streusel mixture.
7. Bake in a 350°F (180°C) oven for 50-60 minutes, or until a toothpick comes out clean. Cool the cake in the pan for 10 minutes, then turn it out onto a plate. Serve warm or cold.

Makes 1 coffee cake.

TO REHEAT: Wrap in foil and heat about 20 minutes at 350°F (180°C).

See photograph on page 69.

  *Bread & Breakfast*

Jalapeño Cheese Muffins

2 cups	flour	500 mL
1 tbsp.	baking powder	15 mL
½ tsp.	baking soda	2 mL
1 tbsp.	white sugar	15 mL
½ tsp.	salt	2 mL
2 cups	grated Cheddar cheese	500 mL
1 tbsp.	finely minced onion	15 mL
1 cup	yogurt OR sour cream	250 mL
¼ cup	melted butter OR margarine	60 mL
2	eggs	2
1-2 tbsp.	finely chopped jalapeño peppers	15-30 mL

1. In a large bowl, mix flour, baking powder, baking soda, sugar and salt. Add cheese and onion and mix with a fork.
2. Whisk yogurt, melted butter, eggs and jalapeños together. Add to dry ingredients. Stir just until evenly moistened.
3. Bake in greased muffin cups at 400°F (200°C) for 15 minutes.

Makes 1 dozen.

Giant Peaches and Cream Muffins

¼ cup	melted butter OR margarine	60 mL
⅓ cup	liquid honey	75 mL
2	eggs, beaten	2
1¼ cups	milk	300 mL
1 tsp.	grated fresh lemon rind	5 mL
1½ cups	100% bran cereal	375 mL
14 oz.	can peaches, drained	398 mL
4 oz.	cream cheese	125 g
2 cups	flour	500 mL
1 tbsp.	baking powder	15 mL
1 tsp.	cinnamon	5 mL
½ tsp.	salt	2 mL

1. Mix melted butter, honey and eggs and beat well. Add milk, lemon rind and bran cereal and mix well.
2. Cube peaches and cream cheese. Stir them into the egg mixture.
3. In a large, separate bowl, combine remaining ingredients. Make a well in center. Stir in the egg mixture, until just moistened.
4. Spoon into prepared ½ cup (125 mL) muffin tins (either greased or lined with paper muffin cups). Muffin cups will be full to overflowing. Bake at 400°F (200°C) for 20-25 minutes.

Makes 12 large muffins. They freeze well.

Cranberry Orange Muffins

This is a delicious light muffin with just a hint of cinnamon.

1 cup	sour cream	250 mL
1½ tsp.	freshly grated orange rind	7 mL
¼ cup	orange juice	60 mL
1	egg	1
⅓ cup	firmly packed brown sugar	75 mL
¼ cup	white sugar	60 mL
¼ cup	butter OR margarine, melted	60 mL
1½ cups	flour	375 mL
2 tsp.	baking powder	10 mL
1 tsp.	baking soda	5 mL
½ tsp.	salt	2 mL
1 tsp.	cinnamon	5 mL
1½ cups	cranberries, fresh, frozen OR dried (page 202)	375 mL

1. In a small bowl, whisk together the sour cream, orange rind, orange juice, egg, the sugars and the butter.
2. In a second bowl, combine the flour, baking powder, baking soda, salt and cinnamon.
3. Add the sour cream mixture to the dry ingredients and stir until it is just combined. Stir in the cranberries.
4. Divide mixture between 12 well-greased, ½-cup (125 mL) muffin tins.
5. Bake at 400°F (200°C) for 15-20 minutes, or until muffins are golden brown and a tester comes out clean.
6. Let muffins cool in pan for 2 minutes, then on cooling rack.

Makes 12 muffins.

Fisherman's Breakfast

Cranberry Streusel Coffee Cake, page 66
Orange Julius, page 45
Crispy Round Oven Fries, page 131
Miniature Oven Omelets, page 73

Fabulous French Toast

The name says it all! The orange butter gives this dish a nice twist.

French Toast:

4	eggs	4
½ cup	milk	125 mL
¼ cup	brown sugar	69 mL
2 tbsp.	orange juice concentrate	30 mL
1 tsp.	grated orange rind	5 mL
1 tsp.	vanilla	5 mL
¼ tsp.	nutmeg	1 mL
½ tsp.	cinnamon	2 mL
8	bread slices	8

Orange Butter:

½ cup	butter	125 mL
1 tsp.	grated orange rind	5 mL
2 tsp.	orange juice concentrate	10 mL
¼ tsp.	vanilla	1 mL
	icing sugar	
	sliced fresh fruit	

1. Preheat oven to 150°F (65°C). (This is just for keeping the toast warm.)
2. In a shallow pan, mix eggs, milk, sugar, orange juice and rind, vanilla and spices.
3. In a separate bowl, mix the ingredients for orange butter. Melt 1 tbsp. (15 mL) of orange butter in a skillet over medium heat.
4. Dip bread, 1 piece at at time, in the egg mixture. Fry it in the orange butter for 1-2 minutes on each side, or until browned. When cooked, transfer toast to a serving dish in the oven.
5. Serve toast with icing sugar, orange butter and an assortment of fresh fruit on the side.

Serves 4-6.

Fisherman on North Knife Lake.

Finnish Oven Pancake

A light and attractive pancake, made without fuss in a baking pan.

3 tbsp.	butter OR margarine	45 mL
3	eggs	3
1 cup	milk	250 mL
1 tsp.	vanilla	5 mL
1 tbsp.	sugar	15 mL
¼ tsp.	salt	1 mL
½ cup	flour	125 mL
½ tsp.	nutmeg	2 mL

1. Preheat oven to 400°F (200°C).
2. Melt butter in a 9 x 13" (23 x 33 cm) baking pan in the oven.
3. Beat the eggs until fluffy. Add milk and vanilla.
4. Add the dry ingredients and beat until smooth.
5. Pour the batter into the prepared pan. Bake for 16-18 minutes, or until a knife inserted in center of the pancake comes out clean. Cut into 6-8 squares and serve.

Serves 2-4, depending on what else is being served with it.

SERVING SUGGESTION: Serve with our Pancake Syrup, page 201, OR fresh fruit and yogurt or sour cream.

Wake-Up Eggs

You can have these eggs any way you like them – hot 'n' spicy or with a hint of sweetness. Either way they are some good!

Sweet Style:

12	bread slices	12
½ cup	maple syrup	125 mL
¼ cup	melted butter OR margarine	60 mL
12	bacon strips, cooked crisp, diced	12
12	eggs	12
	salt and pepper OR DLS* to taste	

For a woman, backseat driving is no different than a man cooking from the dining room table!

Bread & Breakfast

Wake-Up Eggs

Continued

1. Remove the crusts from the bread and flatten with a rolling pin.
2. Mix the maple syrup and melted butter and brush generously over 1 side of the bread.
3. Press each bread slice, syrup-side down, into a large, ungreased muffin cup.
4. Divide the bacon equally among muffin cups.
5. Break 1 egg into each cup and sprinkle with seasonings.
6. Cover with foil and bake at 400°F (200°C) for 15-18 minutes.

Serves 6 -12.

VARIATION: HOT STYLE: Follow directions above but substitute ¼ cup (60 mL) of Louisiana Hot Sauce for the maple syrup.

Miniature Oven Omelets

These little omelets are baked in large muffin tins, making them easy to serve, and fast to bake. The formula we use is 1 tbsp. (15 mL) milk for each egg. We've written the recipe for 12 eggs, but it can be easily adapted for any desired amount.

12	eggs	12
¾ cup	milk	175 mL
½ tsp.	salt	2 mL
1 tsp.	DLS*	5 mL
½ cup	grated cheese	125 mL
2 tbsp.	chopped green pepper	30 mL
¼ cup	chopped tomatoes	60 mL
2 tbsp.	chopped chives OR green onions	30 mL

1. Preheat oven to 350°F (180°C). Spray ½ cup (125 mL) muffin tins (or grease with oil or margarine).
2. Mix all ingredients together and beat with a whisk or beater.
3. Fill prepared muffin tins ¾ full with egg mixture. Bake for 15 minutes, or until omelets are puffed and set. Omelets will sink in the middle when removed from oven. This is normal behavior!

Makes 12 mini-omelets. Serves 6

NOTE: When a knife is inserted in middle of omelets and comes out clean, they are done. Large tart tins may also be used, but they don't hold quite as much of the mixture, so a full recipe will make a few more omelets.

* *Dymond Lake Seasoning. Replace DLS with ¼ tsp. (1 mL) EACH pepper, thyme, oregano, paprika.*

See photograph on page 69.

Baked Eggs and Tomato Casserole

For a special breakfast or brunch, a nice, light egg dish.

1 tbsp.	olive oil	15 mL
1 tbsp.	butter OR margarine	15 mL
6	large eggs	6
⅔ cup	grated Gruyère cheese	150 mL
2	green onions, chopped	2
½ tsp.	dried tarragon OR basil OR 1½ tsp. (7 mL) chopped fresh	2 mL
¼ tsp.	EACH salt and pepper	1 mL
2	medium tomatoes, sliced	2

1. Place oil and butter in an 8" (20 cm) baking dish (round, oval or square) and put it in the oven to melt butter.
2. In a mixing bowl, beat the eggs with a whisk. Stir in cheese, onions and seasonings.
3. Remove the baking dish from the oven and swirl it around to coat it evenly with the oil mixture. Pour in the egg mixture and arrange the tomato slices on top.
4. Bake at 400°F (200°C) for 15-25 minutes, until the eggs are just set. Time will depend on the dish shape. Check the center for doneness.

Serves 4.

Calm, Cool and Collected

(HELEN) Another season was coming to an end at Dymond Lake – or so we thought. The guides had gone home; my daughter Toni and I were almost finished closing up camp, when a radio message arrived that the four fishermen Doug had at North Knife Lake wanted to come to Dymond Lake for a few days of hunting. Since they arrived without an alarm clock, I had to run over to their cabin at 4:30 a.m., in the dark, to wake them up. Knowing that there are often polar bears around, for the first two mornings, in fear and trembling, I took my flashlight and ran as fast as I could to the cabin, banged on the door and ran back to the dining room with my heart just pounding. The third night, when I crawled into bed, I told myself that I was being silly and decided that the next morning I was going to step calmly out on the step, walk serenely over to the cabin, bang on the door and walk back to the dining room. The next morning, I stepped calmly out on the step, swept my flashlight around and there, not twenty feet away, was a polar bear looking right at me. I rushed back into the cabin and slammed the door. My hunters got a late start that morning, and I learned two valuable lessons.

First, "Never let my husband talk me into staying at the lodge with no guides!" Second, always take time to listen to that still, small voice within me. It probably saved my life!

Bacon and Eggs Casserole

When serving a large group for breakfast, here is a simple way to present eggs. This is especially good for buffet-style brunch, or try the smaller version – Brunch for Two.

4	bacon strips	4
18	eggs	18
1 cup	milk	250 mL
1 cup	shredded Cheddar cheese	250 mL
1 cup	sour cream	250 mL
¼ cup	sliced green onion	60 mL
1 tsp.	salt	5 mL
½ tsp.	pepper	2 mL

1. Cook the bacon until crisp, then drain and crumble.
2. Beat the eggs and add the remaining ingredients to them. Pour egg mixture into a greased 9 x 13" (23 x 33 cm) casserole. Sprinkle the bacon on top.
3. Bake, UNCOVERED, at 325°F (160°C) for 40-45 minutes, or until set. Let sit 5 minutes before serving.

Serves 8-10.

Brunch for Two

2	bacon strips	2
4	large eggs	4
¼ cup	milk	60 mL
¼ cup	grated Cheddar cheese	60 mL
¼ cup	sour cream	60 mL
1 tbsp.	sliced chives OR green onions	15 mL
¼ tsp.	salt	1 mL
	pepper	

1. Follow the instructions above, but bake in a small casserole, approximately 6" (15 cm) square or the equivalent, for 30-35 minutes.

Serves 2.

VARIATIONS: PEPPERY BACON AND EGGS CASSEROLE:
For those of you addicted to hot peppers, and there a lot of you, feel free to add chopped jalapeños and a splash of your favorite pepper sauce. Chopped red pepper also adds a great color note. Serve with salsa and a dollop of sour cream to complete the peppery theme.

Crunchy Granola

This recipe was a favorite at Marie's house when the kids were growing up. There was always a supply on hand – except if the supplies had run out during freeze-up and break-up. In those days the northern villages had no air strips, and people were isolated from the outside world until the ice froze or thawed. In any case, Marie ordered her basics in only once a year!

4 cups	rolled oats	1 L
1½ cups	shredded, unsweetened coconut	375 mL
1 cup	wheat germ	250 mL
1 cup	chopped nuts	250 mL
1 cup	sunflower seeds	250 mL
½ cup	sesame seeds	125 mL
½ cup	flax seed	125 mL
½ cup	bran	125 mL
½ cup	oil	125 mL
½ cup	liquid honey	125 mL
½ tsp.	vanilla	2 mL
	raisins, dried berries	

1. Mix together in a large bowl the rolled oats, coconut, wheat germ, nuts, sunflower seeds, sesame seeds, flax seeds and bran.
2. Heat together the oil, honey and vanilla.
3. Add the honey mixture to the dry ingredients and mix well. The mixture will be very dry.
4. Spread granola on 2 ungreased cookie sheet with raised sides and bake at 325°F (160°C), turning every 10 minutes until light brown, about 30 minutes.
5. When cool, add raisins and dried berries, if desired. Store in an airtight container to retain freshness.

Makes 10 cups.

The game warden was walking through the woods one day, when he came across a hunter roasting a bird over an open fire. "That looks like a Bald Eagle," he said. "Yes it is," replied the hunter. "You can't hunt that," exclaimed the warden, "it's an endangered species! But just out of curiosity, what does it taste like?" The hunter, eager to share his superior knowledge, declared, "A little like Peregrine Falcon!"

Midday Madness

Most lunches for the guests at North Knife Lake are shore lunches – freshly caught fish served up by the guides in the Great Outdoors, and leftovers for the staff back at the lodge – but there are times when the weather forces everyone indoors and we are put to the test with our creative ingenuity. It helps to have a good variety of soups to choose from. A lot of the time, our best soups are simply a combination of leftovers – for example, the Wild Rice Lemon Soup, page 89, was inspired by throwing the Lemon Rice Stuffing from Stuffed, Baked Lake Trout "Blueberries & Polar Bears" into some leftover Cream of Wild Rice Soup "Blueberries & Polar Bears". Doesn't sound too appetizing? Wait until you try it! We have made a few adjustments, of course!

Although this section is heavy on soups, don't miss the other lunch ideas. They are all superlative!

Greek Pizza with Herbed Crust

(MARIE) Blending two cultures is not unusual these days, and pizza has become a household word – not like the first time I tasted it at age 5, when my sister and I were invited home by an Italian friend to taste her Mom's pizza pie. Expecting a sweet pie, I quickly decided it was disgusting. How times and tastes change!

Herbed Pizza Crust:

1 cup	warm water	250 mL
1 tbsp.	white sugar	15 mL
1 tsp.	salt	5 mL
1 tbsp.	vegetable OR olive oil	15 mL
½ tsp.	dried oregano OR 1½ tsp. (7 mL) chopped fresh	2 mL
½ tsp.	dried basil OR 1½ tsp. (7 mL) chopped fresh	2 mL
¼ tsp.	dried thyme OR ¾ tsp. (3 mL) chopped fresh	1 mL
2¼ cups	flour (approximately)	550 mL
1 tbsp.	instant yeast*	15 mL

Herbed Tomato Sauce:

5½ oz.	can tomato paste	156 mL
2	garlic cloves, crushed	2
½ tsp.	dried basil OR 1½ tsp. (7 mL) chopped fresh	2 mL
½ tsp.	dried oregano OR 1½ tsp. (7 mL) chopped fresh	2 mL

Spinach Feta Topping:

10 oz.	pkg. frozen spinach, well drained	283 g
1 cup	crumbled feta cheese (or more, to taste)	250 mL
½ cup	black olives, sliced	125 mL
2	tomatoes, quartered and sliced**	2
	onion rings – enough to decorate the top of the pizzas	
2 tbsp.	chopped chives	30 mL

1. In a small bowl, mix all crust ingredients, but add only 1½ cups (375 mL) flour. Add yeast, then add remaining flour, gradually working as much of it into the dough with your hands as you are able. On a floured surface, knead dough for about 5 minutes, until smooth. Divide into 2 halves and shape each into a ball. Let rest for 10 minutes.
2. Grease 2 round pizza pans and press the dough into the pans.
3. Combine the sauce ingredients and spread evenly over the 2 crusts.
4. Place toppings on the pizzas, in the order given.
5. Bake in a 425°F (220°C) oven for 16 minutes. If using 2 shelves, switch pizzas after 8 minutes.

Makes 2 pizzas.

* *See note on Yeast, page 50.*
** *Sun-dried tomatoes are good, too. Reconstitute in boiling water before using, and cut into smaller pieces. Best when combined with fresh tomatoes!*

Hot Chicken Salad with Lemon Dressing

From a creative friend in Northern Manitoba comes this quick and delicious version of a salad you'll want to enjoy with family and guests. Thanks, Donna!

½	head iceberg lettuce (or a mixture of lettuces)	½
3	green onions, chopped	3
1	avocado, sliced	1
¼ cup	sliced almonds, roasted	60 mL
4	boneless and skinless chicken breasts	4
2 tbsp.	vegetable oil	30 mL
1	garlic clove, crushed OR chopped	1
	DLS* OR other peppery meat seasoning	
	salt	

Lemon Dressing**:

⅓ cup	lemon juice (juice of 1 lemon)	75 mL
3 tbsp.	honey	45 mL
1 tsp.	basil vinegar OR any flavor you have on hand	5 mL
1 tsp.	hot mustard OR ½ tsp. (2 mL) mustard powder	5 mL
½ cup	salad dressing OR mayonnaise	125 mL

1. Tear the lettuce into bite-sized pieces and toss it with onion, avocado and almonds. Place in a serving bowl and set aside.
2. Cut the chicken into strips. Fry chicken in oil, with the crushed garlic. Season generously with DLS, or other seasoning, and salt, to taste. After approximately 5 minutes, remove chicken from pan and set aside. (Chicken does not have to be browned.)
3. To the frying pan, add all the lemon dressing ingredients and mix well with a whisk. When warm, return chicken to pan. Reheat and serve warm over the lettuce mixture.

Serves 4.

SERVING SUGGESTION: *Serve with noodles or fettuccine and garlic toast.*

* *Dymond Lake Seasoning*
** *This makes enough dressing for the salad only. If you want to serve the dressing over the noodles as well, double the dressing recipe.*

See photograph on page 87.

My wife told me, if I didn't quit fishing, she would leave me. Lord, I'm going to miss that woman!

Savory Poached Chicken

If you haven't yet discovered the benefits of a poached chicken, you really must. This concept came to me when I was enjoying a particularly moist chicken sandwich in a restaurant – and enquired about how it was cooked. You guessed it — poached! So, I went home and threw a few herbs into a pot of water with a chicken and was rewarded with the results. I know you will enjoy this tasty, low-fat meat, however you decide to serve it.

1	chicken, frying OR roasting, or chicken parts	1
1 tsp.	dried rosemary OR 1 tbsp. (15 mL) chopped fresh	5 mL
1 tsp.	dried thyme OR 1 tbsp. (15 mL) chopped fresh	5 mL
½ tsp.	dried marjoram OR ½ tbsp. (7 mL) chopped fresh	2 mL
1 tsp.	salt	5 mL
1 tsp.	peppercorns	5 mL
1	bay leaf	1

1. Place the chicken in a Dutch oven or suitable saucepan; barely cover the chicken with water. Add seasonings, just bring to a boil, turn down heat, cover and simmer (but do NOT boil) for 2 hours. Skim as necessary.
2. Remove chicken from broth. Remove skin and chicken is ready to slice. Eat hot, or allow chicken to cool for sandwiches or cold lunch meat.

NOTE: Save the broth to use in soup recipes. Chill the broth overnight and skim off the fat.

Croque

Croque is French for crisp or toasted. This crisp, baked loaf has graced many Ladies' Club Meetings in Churchill, Manitoba. Consider it for a special luncheon or a late night "snack".

1 lb.	extra lean ground beef	500 g
½ cup	chopped onion	125 mL
1 tbsp.	prepared mustard	15 mL
8	soda crackers, crushed	8
1	egg	1
½ lb.	mozzarella cheese, grated	250 g
¼ cup	evaporated milk	60 mL
1 tsp.	salt	5 mL
1 tsp.	DLS* or ½ tsp. (2 mL) seasoned pepper	5 mL
1	French loaf	

Croque

Continued

1. Mix all the ingredients together, except the French loaf.
2. Split the French loaf in half lengthwise and spread the meat filling on both halves. Place both halves on a cookie sheet and bake them at 350°F (180°C) for 1 hour. Serve hot from the oven.

Serves 6.

* *Dymond Lake Seasoning*

Incredible Bread & Cheese Surprise

You'll impress your luncheon guests with this one; it's deceptively delicious. For aroma and flavor this one gets the prize. Thanks, Betty!

4 tbsp.	butter OR margarine	60 mL
1	garlic clove, minced	1
6	slices white bread, minus crusts	6
3	eggs	3
1 cup	white wine	250 mL
½ cup	chicken stock	125 mL
1 tbsp.	Worcestershire sauce	15 mL
1 scant tsp.	salt	4 mL
½ tbsp.	Dijon mustard	7 mL
½ tsp.	paprika OR cayenne pepper	2 mL
2 cups	freshly grated Gruyère cheese, (approx. 8 oz. [250g])	500 mL
1	green onion, sliced	1

1. Mix together the butter and garlic. Butter 1 side of each bread slice with the butter mixture. Line a 9 x 13" (23 x 33 cm) baking dish, bottom and sides, with bread, placing slices butter-side down. You will have to cut the bread in half to line the sides.
2. Mix the remaining ingredients together and pour into the lined pan.
3. Bake for 1 hour at 325°F (160°C).

Serves 8.

SERVING SUGGESTION: Serve with Egyptian Salad, page 119, and buns.

NOTE: A 1-pound (500 g) block of cheese will give you 4 cups (1 L) of grated cheese.

All-Vegetable Beet Borscht

(MARIE) This soup is of Mennonite origin, as is testified by the use of dill. I like to cut each vegetable in a different shape, so that when they all turn red, I still know what I'm eating!

½ cup	dry navy beans (optional)	125 mL
6 cups	soup stock, beef OR pork	1.5 L
2 cups	raw OR canned beets, cut in long, fine strips	500 mL
1 cup	sliced carrots	250 mL
1 cup	diced potatoes	250 mL
2 cups	coarsely shredded cabbage	500 mL
1	medium onion, chopped	1
1 cup	tomato juice	250 mL
1	bay leaf	1
1	sprig of dill OR 2 tsp. (10 mL) dillweed	10 mL
2 tsp.	DLS* OR seasoned pepper	10 mL
	salt to taste	
	sour cream for garnish	

1. If you are using dry beans, boil them in 2 cups (500 mL) water for about 1 hour, or until soft. Drain.
2. Put all ingredients (including beans) in a large pot and simmer gently until all the vegetables are tender, about 30 minutes.
3. Add more water, if necessary, to cover the vegetables. Amounts given are not intended to be exact. Add more dill, pepper and salt, to taste. Serve with a tbsp. (15 mL) of sour cream in each bowl of soup.

Serves 4-6.

* *Dymond Lake Seasoning*

Viennese Potato Cream Soup

A thick, rich, creamy soup.

4	medium potatoes, peeled, cubed	4
½ cup	chopped onion	125 mL
½ tsp.	salt	2 mL
1 tsp.	DLS* or ½ tsp. (2 mL) pepper	5 mL
1 cup	strong chicken stock	250 mL
2 cups	milk	500 mL
½ tsp.	dried chopped dillweed OR 1 tbsp. (15 mL) fresh	2 mL
½ tsp.	dried chopped chives OR 1 tbsp. (15 mL) fresh	2 mL
1 cup	sour cream	250 mL

Midday Madness

Viennese Potato Cream Soup

Continued

1. Cook potatoes, onion, salt and DLS* in stock. Don't let it boil dry.
2. Purée the potato mixture in blender or food processor with milk.
3. Add dill, chives and sour cream. Reheat, but do NOT boil. Add milk as needed for desired consistency, and more seasoning, to taste.

Serves 4

* *Dymond Lake Seasoning*

I Didn't Know Anyone Was In Here!

(HELEN) In 1986, when construction had just begun on North Knife Lake Lodge, I convinced Doug that we needed an operational shower room – in a separate building. By late Saturday night the water tank was full, the propane water heater was running, and I went to bed dreaming of a shower on Sunday morning. Now, when you run an operation like North Knife Lake Lodge, it is really like running your own little public works department. You have to have water, sewer, electricity, telephone, road clearance, your own runway and much more. As a result, you are always listening and looking for things that might be a problem and need fixing. After breakfast I headed off to the burning barrel to burn up some of the mountains of burnable materials that are a byproduct of construction. As I passed the shower room, I heard water running. My first thought was, "Oh no, a water line has broken and there is going to be a foot of water in there." I went running up the steps, threw open the door – no water on the floor. But, that didn't stop me, I could still hear water running in the shower. The shower head must have come off. I rushed over to the shower, whipped back the curtain, thrust my hand on the tap and looked up to see Albert, one our carpenters, looking down at me with a very puzzled expression. All he said was "Yes?" Was I embarrassed! All I could think to say was, "I didn't think there was anybody in here." I quickly turned to go and then saw his clothes scattered on the floor and thought, "oh sure – shower running, clothes on the floor and I didn't think there was anybody in here"! It was one of life's more embarrassing moments!

Jeanne's Turkey Chowder

This uses up leftover turkey and potatoes, but it can also be made from scratch.

2 cups	chopped celery	500 mL
1 cup	chopped onion	250 mL
1½ cups	sliced fresh mushrooms OR 10 oz. can (284 mL)	375 mL
½ cup	butter OR margarine	125 mL
3 cups	mashed potatoes	750 mL
7-8 cups	turkey OR chicken stock	1.75-2 L
2-3 cups	cooked, chopped turkey	500-750 mL
14 oz.	can creamed corn	398 mL
13½ oz.	can evaporated milk	385 mL
1 tsp.	ground ginger	5 mL
	DLS* or salt and pepper to taste	

1. In a large soup pot, sauté celery, onions and mushrooms in butter until onions are translucent. Add mashed potatoes and heat until softened. Gradually add broth, stirring to break up the mashed potatoes.
2. Add the remaining ingredients. Reheat and serve. This freezes well.

Serves 8-10.

NOTE: *If making from scratch, boil turkey parts and reserve the stock. Add potato liquid to stock to make 7-8 cups (1.75-2 L).*

* *Dymond Lake Seasoning*

Soup Après Ski

There are times when a quick fix is what is needed. Keep bean and bacon soup on hand and dress it up to warm your insides when you come in from the cold.

4	bacon slices OR garlic sausage	4
½ cup	chopped onion	125 mL
10 oz.	can bean and bacon soup	284 mL
10 oz.	can water	284 mL
14 oz.	can tomatoes, puréed	398 mL
	cayenne, Tabasco OR salsa to taste. (2 tbsp. [30 mL] HOT salsa gives it a real BITE)	

1. Cut the bacon in small pieces and fry it with the onion. Drain and discard drippings. (I even rinse it with hot water!)
2. Heat the soup, water and tomatoes in a saucepan. Add the bacon and onions. Add seasonings as desired.

Serves 3-4.

Chunky Corn Chowder

In many parts of the world, corn is a staple. In fact, the Indian word for corn means"our life". No wonder corn chowder is a soup classic.

6 tbsp.	butter OR margarine	90 mL
2	small potatoes, peeled and diced	2
2	celery stalks, finely chopped	2
1	small green pepper, finely chopped	1
1	small onion, finely chopped	1
1½ tsp.	salt	7 mL
2 tbsp.	EACH flour and paprika	30 mL
1½ cups	chicken stock	375 mL
2 cups	frozen corn	500 mL
4 cups	whole milk OR cream (fresh or canned)	1 L

1. Melt butter or margarine in a large saucepan over medium heat. Sauté potatoes, celery, green pepper and onion until vegetables are tender, about 10 minutes. Add salt.
2. Stir in flour and paprika until well blended. Add stock, stirring constantly over medium heat until smooth and thickened, about 5 minutes.
3. Stir in the corn and milk. Cook, stirring frequently, until corn is tender and mixture is heated through, about 10 minutes.

Serves 4-6.

Snowmobiling Fun???

(HELEN) Doug, being very much an outdoor enthusiast, was amongst the first to get involved in the snowmobiling craze in Churchill. One bright Saturday, he persuaded me to leave the girls with my sister so I could come with him and share in the "fun". There was a catch – we only had one machine and since Doug had to do the driving, he had borrowed a sled for me! It was the type of sled that was usually pulled by dogs and I was to stand on the back of it. This involved a bit of skill and I was going to have to "lean" in the right direction at the right time in order to stay upright. Well, I must have failed Leaning 101 because I was dumped off that sleigh at least 20 times. One time my foot got caught in one of the ropes and I was dragged for what seemed like half a mile, although it was likely much less, before Doug noticed that there was a bit of a drag on his machine! When I loudly proclaimed that this stupid snowmobiling was NOT fun and I was never going to have anything to do with it again, Doug realized something had to be done to save the day. So, when he had confirmed that I was indeed unhurt he immediately suggested that I should take a turn driving. Suddenly the machine wasn't as difficult to handle as he had first led me to believe. Well that put a whole new light on things. I fell in love with the sport – as long as I was driving. As for Doug on the sled – he had obviously passed his Leaning 101 because as hard as I tried for the rest of the afternoon I was unable to dump him!

Creamy Zucchini (Or Squash) Soup

It's always nice to find something to do with all that zucchini you harvest in the fall. This soup can be made with fresh or frozen zucchini so enjoy it all year round. We also make it with other varieties of orange squash, such as Hubbard or butternut, and it is equally delicious.

8 cups	zucchini slices, (unpeeled, if young and tender enough)	2 L
1 cup	chopped onion	250 mL
1 cup	strong chicken stock	250 mL
1 cup	whole milk OR cream (fresh OR canned)	250 mL
1 tsp.	DLS* or seasoned pepper (or more, to taste)	5 mL
½ tsp.	salt	2 mL

1. Cook the zucchini slices and onion in stock until vegetables are soft, about 10-15 minutes. Put it all through a blender. Return the mixture to the pot and add milk and seasonings.
2. Heat thoroughly and serve.

Serves 4.

VARIATIONS: Other kinds of squash need to be peeled and the seeds removed. Try a mixture of squashes if you are fortunate enough to have a few varieties on hand. Spices that are especially good with the orange winter squashes are mace and ginger, try ½ tsp. (2 mL) of each. A tbsp. (15 mL) of brown sugar and a dash of cayenne also complement the rich flavor of winter squash.

* *Dymond Lake Seasoning*

Goose Facts – What Is All The Racket About?

Canada geese utter 10 different vocalizations, so they have a language with which they communicate. During migration, geese honk from behind to encourage those up front to keep up their speed.

Midday Madness – Main Course Salad & Buns

Hot Chicken Salad with Lemon Dressing, page 79
Crunchy Brown Buns, page 60

Wild Rice Lemon Soup

The tang of lemon adds a complementary zest to wild rice. This soup is also versatile; you can go vegetarian or add chicken or fish for equally good results.

½ cup	raw wild rice	125 mL
6 cups	chicken stock	1.5 L
½ tsp.	salt	2 mL
½ tsp.	dried rosemary* OR 1 tbsp. (15 mL) chopped fresh	2 mL
¼ tsp.	dried thyme* OR 1½ tsp. (7 mL) chopped fresh	1 mL
1 tsp.	DLS** or ½ tsp. (2 mL) pepper	5 mL
½-1 tsp.	freshly grated lemon peel	2-5 mL
1 tbsp.	lemon juice	15 mL
¼ cup	butter OR margarine	60 mL
½ cup	chopped onion	125 mL
½ cup	chopped celery	125 mL
2 tbsp.	chopped green pepper	30 mL
1 cup	sliced fresh mushrooms	250 mL
1 cup	chicken OR fish in bite-sized pieces, raw OR cooked (optional)	250 mL
	fresh chives	

1. Place wild rice in a saucepan with chicken broth, spices, lemon rind and juice. Bring to a boil, reduce heat and simmer for 1 hour, or until the rice is very tender.
2. In a frying pan melt the margarine. Sauté the onion and celery for 5 minutes over medium heat. Add the remaining vegetables and sauté for another 5 minutes, or until tender.
3. Add the vegetables to the cooked rice. If using, add raw or cooked chicken or fish. Simmer for 5 minutes and serve. Garnish with chives.

Serves 6.

* *If fresh herbs are not available, substitute 1 tbsp. (15 mL) of crushed dried herbs for ⅓ cup (75 mL) chopped fresh herbs. The general rule is 1 tsp. (5 mL) crushed dried herbs equals 2 tbsp. (30 mL) chopped fresh.*
** *Dymond Lake Seasoning*

God Bless this bunch
As we munch our lunch.

Shore lunch with Mike Boll, guide and cook.

Orchard Soup

(MARIE) Part of marketing a cookbook is being on the road a lot. This curried apple and potato soup was served to my husband, Gary, when friends rescued him from a lonely Thanksgiving. He loved it, and brought the recipe home!

1 cup	chopped onions	250 mL
1 cup	chopped celery	250 mL
1	potato, peeled and chopped	1
1	cucumber, peeled, seeded and chopped	1
1	large, tart apple, peeled, cored and chopped	1
3 cups	chicken stock	750 mL
½ cup	light cream OR evaporated milk	125 mL
½ tsp.	curry powder	2 mL
	salt and pepper	
	chopped chives	

1. In a large saucepan, combine first 6 ingredients. Bring to a boil, reduce heat, cover and simmer 20-30 minutes, until vegetables are soft.
2. Purée in food processor or blender. Return the purée to the saucepan. Stir in milk, curry powder, salt and pepper, to taste.
3. To serve, reheat and sprinkle with chives.

Serves 8.

Gazpacho

This salad-lover's soup is served cold. It's best on a hot summer day, served with nothing but French bread and a bottle of white wine. We've persuaded a lot of people to try black olives when serving this soup and, surprise! they like them!

2x28 oz.	tins tomatoes, coarsely chopped	2x796 mL
1	English cucumber, quartered and sliced	1
1½ cups	Spanish OR Greek black olives, sliced OR whole	398 mL
2	green peppers, halved and sliced	2
1	Spanish (sweet) onion, sliced	1
4	garlic cloves, minced	4
1 tbsp.	chopped fresh parsley, OR ½ tsp. (2 mL) dried	15 mL
pinch	dried marjoram	pinch
⅓ cup	olive oil	75 mL
3 tbsp.	red wine vinegar	45 mL
	salt and pepper to taste	

1. Mix all together and chill until serving time. What could be easier?

Serves 6 people.

SERVING SUGGESTION: Throw a few ice cubes in the serving bowl. They really don't dilute the taste, and they keep the soup really cold. If you haven't tried cold soup before, you'll be sure to enjoy this one! Garlic croûtons are also a great accompaniment to this classic soup.

Stop & Snack Awhile

Most of these recipes have been around for a long time. They are favorites of ours, yours, of whoever chose to share them with us. They have passed the test of our most severe critics – family and staff – and are deemed worthy to be tasted by guests and patrons alike. Even at this time, there are probably some of these snacks stored away in a freezer at North Knife Lake. They are put there at the end of each season, when it is cold enough to remain frozen after the electricity is turned off; and they await the arrival of the first staff members who come to open up in the Spring. That isn't quite what I meant when I said these recipes had been around for a long time – but the staff are mighty happy to devour them! From holiday favorites to lunch box cookies, we are happy to pass them on to you.

Almond Ice-Box Cookies

Marie has had this recipe for years but she was holding out on us. She finally brought it up to the lake with her this past season and we can't seem to keep them in the cookie tins. A crisp, snappy, almond cookie, these are simple and delicious.

1 cup	softened butter OR margarine	250 mL
½ cup	brown sugar	125 mL
½ cup	white sugar	125 mL
2 cups	flour	500 mL
½ tsp.	baking powder	2 mL
¾ cup	blanched split almonds	175 mL

1. In a mixing bowl, cream together the butter and sugars.
2. Add flour, baking powder and almonds. Mix very well.
3. Form the dough into 3 or 4 rolls, and wrap each in waxed paper. You may have to press the dough together with your hands. Chill in the refrigerator for 1-2 hours.
4. Slice the rolls in ⅜" (1 cm) slices. Place slices on an ungreased cookie sheet. (If cookies crumble a little when cutting, just push them together on the cookie sheet – they will bake just fine.) Bake at 350°F (180°C) for 10 minutes. Remove cookies to a rack and let cool.

Makes 4-5 dozen cookies.

Chewy Chocolate Chip Cookies

Helen's daughter, Shari, our resident cookie chef, has given this cookie her seal of approval. She's the expert! The secret to a chewy cookie is under baking.

1 cup	butter OR margarine	250 mL
1½ cups	sugar	375 mL
2	eggs	2
1 tsp.	vanilla	5 mL
1 tbsp.	water	15 mL
2½ cups	flour	625 mL
1 tsp.	baking powder	5 mL
1½ tsp.	baking soda	7 mL
½ tsp.	salt	2 mL
1½ cups	rolled oats	375 mL
1½ cups	chocolate chips*	375 mL

Stop & Snack Awhile

Chewy Chocolate Chip Cookies

Continued

1. Cream together the butter and sugar. Add the eggs, 1 at a time, beating well after each. Add the vanilla and water and beat well.
2. Mix the flour, baking powder, baking soda and salt and add to creamed mixture. Add the oats and chocolate chips.
3. Roll into a ball or drop by tablespoonfuls (15 mL) onto a greased cookie pan. Bake in a 375°F (190°C) oven for 10 minutes. Cookies will still be moist and soft. Allow to cool slightly before removing from the pan.

Makes 3-4 dozen cookies.

* *Substitute M+M's (large or baking size) or Smarties for chocolate chips OR reduce chocolate chips to 1 cup (250 mL) and add 1 cup (250 mL) dried cranberries.*

Double Whammy Cookies

Are there many kids (big or little) who don't like chocolate and peanut butter? Better teach them how to make this one themselves 'cause they'll be begging you for more!

1 cup	flour	250 mL
½ cup	cocoa	125 mL
2 tsp.	baking soda	10 mL
1 tsp.	baking powder	5 mL
¾ cup	softened butter OR margarine	175 mL
½ cup	peanut butter	125 mL
1 cup	white sugar	250 mL
2	eggs	2
1 cup	semisweet chocolate chips	250 mL
1 cup	peanut butter chips	250 mL

1. In a small bowl, combine flour, cocoa, baking soda and baking powder.
2. In a large bowl, cream together the butter and peanut butter. Add sugar and eggs, and beat well. Add the flour mixture and both kinds of chips. Stir until well combined.
3. Drop by teaspoonfuls (5 mL) on an ungreased cookie sheet. Do not press down. Bake at 350°F (180°C) for 10-12 minutes.

Makes 3-4 dozen.

Chocolate Nut Chip Cookies

Chocolate chip cookies are such favorites; it never hurts to have several varieties. We have a couple that we use all the time, but we're game to try another.

1⅔ cups	flour	400 mL
⅔ cup	cocoa	150 mL
1 tsp.	baking soda	5 mL
½ tsp.	salt	2 mL
1 cup	butter OR margarine OR shortening	250 mL
¾ cup	lightly packed brown sugar	175 mL
½ cup	white sugar	125 mL
1	egg	1
2 tbsp.	water OR milk	30 mL
2 tsp.	vanilla	10 mL
1 cup	white chocolate chips	250 mL
1 cup	milk chocolate chips (no imitations!)	250 mL
1½ cups	coarsely chopped pecans (or other nuts)	375 mL

1. Combine flour, cocoa, baking soda and salt in a bowl.
2. Cream butter and sugars. Add egg, water and vanilla and beat until light and creamy. Add dry ingredients; mix well. Stir in chips and nuts.
3. Drop by heaping spoonfuls on an ungreased cookie sheet. Press down lightly. Bake at 375°F (190°C) for 7-9 minutes. DO NOT overbake! Let cool slightly before removing to a cooling rack.

Makes 3½ dozen cookies.

Hammer and Chisel Cookies

Layne, a young, adventuresome friend, named these cookies for the method she used to get them off the pan! You won't need a hammer or chisel to eat them!

1 cup	butter OR margarine	250 mL
¾ cup	brown sugar	175 mL
½ cup	white sugar	125 mL
1	egg	1
1½ tsp.	vanilla	7 mL
2 cups	flour	500 mL
1 tsp.	baking soda	5 mL
¼ tsp.	salt	1 mL
1 cup	semisweet chocolate chips OR chunks	250 mL
1 cup	toffee bits* or quartered caramels	250 mL
½ cup	chopped pecans OR walnuts	125 mL

Stop & Snack Awhile

Hammer and Chisel Cookies

Continued

1. With an electric mixer, cream butter, sugars, egg and vanilla in a large bowl, until light and creamy.
2. Combine the flour, baking soda and salt. Add to creamed mixture and mix until blended. Stir in chocolate, toffee and nuts.
3. Drop by heaping spoonfuls onto a greased baking sheet. Bake in a pre-heated 375°F (190°C) oven for 10-12 minutes, or until light golden brown.
4. Remove from baking sheet WHILE STILL WARM and cool on a rack.

Makes 3 dozen.

* *Look in the baking supplies section of your grocery store.*

Crispy Coconut Cookies

This old standby often gets passed up in favor of chocolate and raisins and things like that. It deserves a second chance.

1 cup	melted butter OR margarine	250 mL
½ cup	white sugar	125 mL
½ cup	brown sugar	125 mL
1	egg, beaten	1
1½ cups	flour	375 mL
1 tsp.	baking soda	5 mL
1 tsp.	baking powder	5 mL
½ tsp.	salt	2 mL
1 cup	rolled oats	250 mL
¾ cup	shredded coconut (sweetened OR unsweetened)	175 mL
1 tsp.	vanilla	5 mL
1 tsp.	coconut extract (optional)	5 mL

1. In a large mixing bowl, beat together melted butter, sugars and egg. Add flour, baking soda, baking powder and salt. Mix well. Stir in the oats, coconut and flavorings.
2. Drop dough by heaping spoonfuls on an ungreased cookie sheet. Press down lightly with a fork. Bake at 350°F (180°C) for 10-15 minutes. Cool slightly, then remove to a rack.

Makes 2-3 dozen cookies.

New Year's Cookies

This is a traditional Mennonite cookie though some of us might call it a doughnut. You must eat these before making that New Year's resolution to lose weight!

1 cup	warm water	250 mL
1 cup	half and half cream OR canned milk	250 mL
4	eggs	4
2 tbsp.	butter, melted	30 mL
¼ tsp.	ginger	1 mL
pinch	salt	pinch
6 cups	flour	1.5 L
1 tbsp.	instant yeast*	15 mL
3 cups	raisins	750 mL
	vegetable oil for deep-frying	
	icing sugar for dusting	

1. Mix the first 4 ingredients and add ginger, salt, 3 cups (750 mL) flour, instant yeast and raisins. Work in remainder of flour with a wooden spoon or dough hook until mixture is a fairly thick batter. (This should not be as firm as bread dough.)
2. Let rise in a warm place until doubled in bulk, about 1 hour.
3. Drop by heaping tablespoonfuls (30 mL) into deep hot oil, about 350°F (180°C), and fry until golden brown, about 5 minutes. Remove with a slotted spoon; drain on a rack. Dust with icing sugar before serving.

Makes 7 dozen.

* *See note on YEAST, page 50.*

Couldn't-Be-Easier Almond Squares

Very easy and very, very good!

	graham wafers	
1 cup	sliced almonds	250 mL
1 cup	butter OR margarine	250 mL
⅔ cup	brown sugar	150 mL

1. Lay the graham wafers, side by side, in an ungreased 10 x 15" (25 x 38 cm) jelly-roll pan, with raised sides, to completely cover the surface. Sprinkle sliced almonds evenly over graham wafers.
2. In a saucepan, bring butter and brown sugar to a boil and boil 2 minutes. Pour evenly over wafers.
3. Bake at 350°F (180°C) for 2 minutes. Turn heat down to 300°F (150°C) and bake 8 minutes more.
4. Let sit for 10 minutes; cut while warm, place on cooling rack.

Makes 30 squares.

  Stop & Snack Awhile

Lemon Love Notes

A delicious, refreshing, lemon-laced bar!

½ cup	butter OR margarine	125 mL
1 cup	flour	250 mL
¼ cup	icing sugar	60 mL
1 cup	white sugar	250 mL
2 tbsp.	flour	30 mL
½ tsp.	baking powder	2 mL
2	eggs, beaten	2
2 tbsp.	lemon juice	30 mL
2 tsp.	grated lemon rind	10 mL
	icing sugar	

1. Combine the first 3 ingredients in a bowl. Mix until crumbly. Press into an ungreased 8" (20 cm) square cake pan. Bake at 350°F (180°C) for 15 minutes. Cool in the pan on a rack.
2. Combine sugar, 2 tbsp. (30 mL) flour and baking powder in a bowl. Add eggs, lemon juice and rind. Mix well. Pour over cooled crust.
3. Bake at 350°F (180°C) for 25 minutes. Cool in the pan on a rack. (The top puffs up when baking, but will fall while cooling.)
4. Sprinkle with icing sugar. Cut in 2" (5 cm) squares.

Makes 16 squares.

Rock Star in The Bush

Marie's son, Todd, came to work for us in 1987, which was the year we opened the new lodge at North Knife Lake. Todd was a young man of eighteen whose ambition was to be a "Rock Star". He arrived with his guitar and plans for spending all of his spare time practicing. Our days started with breakfast at five and ended – well, kind of whenever. Todd's duties consisted of combing the beaches with a wheelbarrow and shovel, collecting gravel for the cement work; hammering nails with Len, the carpenter; holding a heavy sander above his head for hours at a time, sanding all the beams in the lodge. In other words, it was heavy, hard work. We had breakfast at five and a coffee break about nine. Todd would walk in, gulp down his juice and a handful of cookies, plop down in the only comfy chair in the place and immediately fall asleep. He would sleep until coffee break was over, jump up and get right back to work. This scene was repeated at lunch, afternoon coffee and supper. After a few weeks of this regime, he was lamenting the fact that he wasn't getting in any guitar practice. In fact, whenever he started to play he fell asleep! I sympathized but assured him that the groupies were going to love all the muscles he was developing with his hard work. He assured me that I was wrong, that groupies prefer wimps.

Todd never did find time to do much practicing that summer but I am pleased to report that it didn't seriously harm his career. He is now lead guitarist at the "Country Tonite" theatre in Branson, Missouri.

Stop & Snack Awhile

Lemon Raspberry Squares

Raspberry lovers unite. This is a delicious way to use up some of that raspberry jam if you have an abundance. If you don't have any homemade, store-bought will do. That's what we have to use. We do have raspberry bushes at North Knife Lake but to date we have harvested only 2-3 cups a year.

1½ cups	flour	375 mL
½ cup	icing sugar	125 mL
¾ cup	butter OR margarine	175 mL
½ cup	raspberry jam*	125 mL
1½ cups	white sugar	375 mL
3 tbsp.	flour	45 mL
1 tsp.	baking powder	5 mL
4	eggs	4
½ cup	lemon juice	125 mL

Lemon Glaze:

½ cup	icing sugar	125 mL
1 tbsp.	melted butter OR margarine	15 mL
1 tbsp.	lemon juice	15 mL

1. Combine 1½ cups (375 mL) flour and the icing sugar. Cut in butter with a pastry blender until crumbly. Press into a greased, 9 x 13" (23 x 33 cm) pan. Bake at 350°F (180°C) for 15-18 minutes, until golden.
2. Heat the jam on the stove or in the microwave until melted. Spread over baked crust.
3. Combine sugar, 3 tbsp. (45 mL) flour and baking powder. Add eggs and lemon juice and mix with a whisk or beater until well blended. Pour over raspberry layer.
4. Bake for 20-25 minutes, just until set. Let cool slightly.
5. Combine glaze ingredients until smooth. Spread on the cooled cake.

Makes 30 squares or more.

* *OR you can use ¾ cup (175 mL) cranberry sauce, or more, to cover cake with as thin a layer as possible.*

Stop & Snack Awhile

Cranberry Squares

Helen's sister, Patti, has been making these squares every Christmas for as long as they can remember. They are a family favorite.

½ cup	butter OR margarine, softened	125 mL
2 tsp.	icing sugar	10 mL
1 cup	flour	250 mL
2	eggs	2
1 cup	white sugar	250 mL
⅓ cup	flour	75 mL
1 tsp.	baking powder	5 mL
¼ tsp.	salt	1 mL
1 tsp.	almond flavoring	5 mL
⅓ cup	chopped raisins	75 mL
⅓ cup	chopped almonds	75 mL
⅓ cup	desiccated coconut	75 mL
⅔ cup	cranberry sauce	150 mL

Lemon Butter Icing:

¼ cup	butter OR margarine	60 mL
1½ cups	icing sugar	375 mL
3 tbsp.	lemon juice	45 mL
½ tsp.	grated lemon rind	2 mL

1. Mix butter, icing sugar and 1 cup (250 mL) flour together and spread in the bottom of a greased, 9 x 13" (23 x 33 cm) pan.
2. Beat eggs thoroughly then add sugar, ⅓ cup (75 mL) flour, baking powder, salt and almond flavoring, mixing well. Stir in the raisins, almonds, coconut and cranberry sauce.
3. Spread the cranberry mixture over the crust. Bake at 350°F (180°C) for 40 minutes. Cool on a rack.
4. When the square is cooled, beat together the ingredients for the Lemon Butter Icing until smooth. Spread icing over the cooled square.

Makes 35 squares.

As usual, the avid fisherman was boring his friends with his angling tales. "Knock it off, will you?" said a companion. "Don't you ever think about anything except fishing? Don't you ever think about hockey or women?" "Sure I do! Only last night I dreamed I was all alone in a canoe with Farah Fawcett-Majors." "Hey, Hey! How'd you make out?" "Terrific! I caught a twelve-pound trout!"

Boreal Forest Cranberry Brownies

Marie came up with these one day when she was looking for a way to combine chocolate and cranberries. We are sure you will agree it is a keeper.

1⅓ cups	flour	325 mL
1 tsp.	baking powder	5 mL
½ tsp.	salt	2 mL
1 cup	butter OR margarine	250 mL
1 cup	cocoa	250 mL
2 cups	white sugar	500 mL
4	eggs	4
1½ tsp.	vanilla	7 mL
1 tsp.	almond extract	5 mL
1 cup	cranberries, fresh OR frozen	250 mL
½ cup	chopped walnuts	125 mL

1. Combine the flour, baking powder and salt in a bowl.
2. Melt butter in a large saucepan. Remove it from the heat. Stir in the cocoa. Add sugar, eggs, vanilla and almond extract, and stir until blended.
3. Stir this mixture into the dry ingredients. Add the cranberries and nuts and mix just until blended.
4. Pour the batter into a greased 9 x 13" (23 x 33 cm) pan. Bake at 350°F (180°C), 30-35 minutes. Cool completely.
5. Ice with Chocolate Cranberry Icing, below.

Chocolate Cranberry Icing

3 tbsp.	butter OR margarine	45 mL
¼ cup	cocoa	60 mL
¼ tsp.	almond extract	1 mL
¼ cup	cranberry sauce*	60 mL
2 tbsp.	cranberry juice OR water	30 mL
2 cups	icing sugar	500 mL

1. Melt the butter in small saucepan. Remove from heat and stir in cocoa and almond extract. Add the cranberry sauce and cranberry juice and stir well. Add the icing sugar and mix until well blended.

* See "Blueberries & Polar Bears" page 198 OR replace the sauce with cranberry juice, adding it gradually to desired consistency.

Stop & Snack Awhile

Fudge Nut Bars

Similar to date squares, but with a fudge filling, these bars will be gobbled up by chocolate lovers. This recipe makes quite a large amount.

Base and Topping:

1 cup	butter OR margarine	250 mL
2 cups	brown sugar, firmly packed	500 mL
2	eggs	2
2 tsp.	vanilla	10 mL
2½ cups	flour	625 mL
1 tsp.	baking soda	5 mL
1 tsp.	salt	5 mL
3 cups	quick rolled oats	750 mL

Fudge Filling:

2 cups	semisweet chocolate chips	500 mL
1 cup	sweetened condensed milk	250 mL
2 tbsp.	butter OR margarine	30 mL
½ tsp.	salt	2 mL
1 cup	chopped walnuts	250 mL
2 tsp.	vanilla	10 mL

1. To make base and topping, cream together butter and sugar in a bowl until light and fluffy. Beat in the eggs and vanilla.
2. Sift together the flour, baking soda and salt. Add with oats to butter mixture and mix well. Spread ⅔ of dough in a greased, 10 x 15" (25 x 38 cm) jelly-roll pan.
3. Combine chocolate chips, condensed milk, butter and salt in a glass measuring cup or bowl. Microwave on medium heat for 4 minutes, or until melted, stirring once after 3 minutes, or melt over water in a double boiler. Add walnuts and 2 tsp. vanilla. Spread over the dough.
4. Dot remaining ⅓ of dough over fudge filling, covering as best you can. This does not have to be a solid layer.
5. Bake at 350°F (180°C) for 25 minutes. Cool in the pan on a rack. Cut into small bars.

Makes 40-50 bars (but they disappear quickly).

Old-Fashioned Raisin Bars

From Helen's mother-in-law, Jeanne, comes a family favorite.

1 cup	butter OR margarine	250 mL
1 cup	white sugar	250 mL
2 cups	flour	500 mL
2 tsp.	baking powder	10 mL
1	egg, beaten	1

Raisin Filling:

1½ tbsp.	cornstarch	22 mL
1 cup	cold water	250 mL
2 cups	raisins	500 mL
2 tbsp.	lemon juice	30 mL
½ cup	white sugar	125 mL
1 tbsp.	butter OR margarine	15 mL

1. Mix together the butter, sugar, flour and baking powder. Add the beaten egg to make a soft dough.
2. Spread half the dough in a greased 9 x 13" (23 x 33 cm) pan.
3. To make the filling, mix cornstarch with a little of the cold water, until it is smooth. Add the rest of the water and all the other ingredients. Heat and stir until it starts to boil. Keep stirring until thickened.
4. Spread raisin filling on base. Crumble the remaining dough on top.
5. Bake at 375°F (190°C) for 30 minutes.

Makes 24 squares.

Pecan Pie Squares

If you like pecan pie, you will love these squares – no fussing with pastry.

1 cup	butter OR margarine	250 mL
¼ cup	icing sugar	60 mL
3 cups	flour	750 mL

Pecan Filling:

½ cup	butter OR margarine, melted	125 mL
½ cup	white sugar	125 mL
1 cup	golden corn syrup	250 mL
½ tsp.	salt	2 mL
1 tbsp.	vanilla	15 mL
3 tbsp.	flour	45 mL
3	eggs	3
2 cups	coarsely chopped pecans	500 mL

Pecan Pie Squares

Continued

1. To prepare the base, cream together the butter and sugar. Blend in flour. It will be crumbly.
2. Pat down crumbs in an ungreased 9 x 13" (23 x 33 cm) pan.
3. Bake in a 350°F (180°C) oven for 5 minutes.
4. To make the filling, pour melted butter into a mixing bowl. Add sugar, syrup, salt, vanilla, flour and eggs and beat well. Fold in pecans.
5. Pour the filling over the baked base. Return pan to oven and bake for 40 minutes more, or until the center is set. Cool to room temperature before cutting. May also be served well chilled.

Makes 24 squares.

All Bush Pilots Must Be Crazy

When we were building the lodge, all the material was flown in by DC3 and landed on the ice. This was a fairly common practice in the north for many years, but it is slowly being phased out as more and more runways are built. Our runway was just a dream for Doug at that time. So on to the ice everything went. The job of getting it off the ice was done on big komatiks pulled by snowmobiles, ATV's and a very old Ford tractor. As long as the ice was still frozen to the shore this task went very smoothly. But as May wore on more and more water opened up between the shore and the hard ice. The men had to build bridges that got longer and more precarious every day. Thirteen DC3 loads of building material and equipment were eventually brought to shore – not without a few close calls, but one snowmobile was still sitting out there. After much discussion, Doug decided it would have to be driven off, and that since no one there had done it before, he had better take the first plunge. The staff gathered, cameras in hand, to record the big event. Far out on the ice, Doug climbed on the machine, drove it around an island to pick up speed, and to get up his nerve, then he came roaring straight for us. He left the ice, skipped neatly across 100 yards (91.4 m) of water and came to a stop outside the pilot's cabin! He barely got his feet wet!

The next year, there was ice on the lake once again when our first guests arrived and the snowmobile was once again sitting a good way off from shore. It was the main topic of conversation amongst the guests at dinner their first night. Doug didn't let on that he had dealt with this problem before, but just told them that he supposed he would have to try to drive it off the next morning, though he would do so with some apprehension. At 7:30 a.m. the guests were all there to watch the spectacle. While Doug was warming up the machine, way out on the ice, and all the fishermen were standing on the dock with their cameras ready, I heard one of the guests say to the group, "all bush pilots must be crazy." I laughed and agreed with him. Once again, Doug brought the machine across, barely getting his feet wet. The question was asked, "How far will a snow machine travel on water before sinking?" Bush pilots may be crazy, but they're not that crazy!

Caramel Popcorn

A "keep-it-on-hand" treat. BUT to keep it on hand, you'll have to hide it! (Even from yourself!) WE DO!

¾ cup	popping corn (unpopped)	175 mL
2 cups	salted peanuts	500 mL

Caramel Sauce:

1 cup	butter or margarine	250 mL
2 cups	packed brown sugar	500 mL
½ cup	corn syrup	125 mL
1 tsp.	salt	5 mL
1 tsp.	vanilla	5 mL
½ tsp.	baking soda	2 mL

1. You'll need a roasting pan to stir this in. Start by popping the corn. Place it in the roasting pan, checking to make sure that none of the unpopped kernels are included. Add salted peanuts to the popcorn.
2. To make the sauce, combine the butter, sugar, corn syrup and salt in a LARGE saucepan. This is important because when you add the baking soda in the next step, it may overflow the pan, and you wouldn't be happy! Heat and stir, over medium heat, until boiling. Boil without stirring for 5 minutes.
3. Stir in vanilla and baking soda. Immediately pour this mixture over the popcorn. Mix well to coat all pieces.
4. Spread on 2 ungreased baking sheets. Jelly roll pans are good. You need pans with raised edges, so that you don't lose the caramel corn when you stir it! You may have to improvise.
5. Bake at 250°F (135°C) for 1 hour, STIRRING EVERY 15 MINUTES.
6. Cool thoroughly. Break apart the Caramel Popcorn and store in plastic bags or containers. Munch out!

Makes 8 quarts (8 L).

  *Stop & Snack Awhile*

Cranberry Orange Loaf

(MARIE) Sandy, who was with us at Dymond Lake, provided us with this wonderful, moist version of a popular recipe. When it calls for orange, she takes it all the way – no grating or peeling here! Helen and I, however, had a serious disagreement about this recipe. She likes cranberries and raisins, and I like cranberries and blueberries. You'll have to decide for yourselves which is best!

2 cups	flour	500 mL
1 cup	white sugar	250 mL
½ tsp.	salt	2 mL
1½ tsp.	baking powder	7 mL
½ tsp.	baking soda	2 mL
1	whole orange cut into ¼" (1 cm) pieces (approx. 1 cup [250 mL])	1
1 cup	cranberries, fresh, frozen OR dried (page 202)	250 mL
½ cup	blueberries OR raisins (optional)	125 mL
1	egg, beaten	1
¼ cup	melted butter OR margarine	60 mL
¾ cup	orange juice	175 ml

Orange Glaze: (optional)

¼ cup	white sugar	60 mL
1	orange, juice of	1

1. In a large mixing bowl, mix flour, sugar, salt, baking powder and baking soda.
2. Wash the orange, and cut it into small cubes leaving the skin on. Remove the pits. Add the orange to the flour mixture, along with the cranberries and blueberries or raisins.
3. Combine the egg, melted butter and orange juice. Add to dry ingredients and mix just until moist.
4. Place dough in a greased 4½ x 8½" (11 x 21 cm) loaf pan. Bake at 350°F (180°C) for 1 hour. Let sit for 10 minutes, then turn out on a rack to cool. If glazing, combine orange juice with sugar. Pour over loaf as soon as it is removed from the oven. Let cool in pan.

Makes 1 loaf.

Spicy Pumpkin Loaf

Very moist, very spicy and very easy. Double the recipe and keep one in your freezer.

1½ cups	flour	375 mL
1 tsp.	baking powder	5 mL
1 tsp.	baking soda	5 mL
½ tsp.	salt	2 mL
1 tsp.	cinnamon	5 mL
½ tsp.	ground cloves	2 mL
¾ tsp.	ground ginger	3 mL
½ tsp.	ground nutmeg	2 mL
2	eggs	2
¾ cup	white sugar	175 mL
¼ cup	corn syrup	60 mL
½ cup	vegetable oil	125 mL
1 cup	canned pumpkin	250 mL
½ cup	raisins	125 mL
½ cup	chopped walnuts	125 mL

1. Combine all ingredients and mix well, using an electric mixer.
2. Turn into a greased 4½ x 8½" (11 x 21 cm) loaf pan and bake at 325°F (160°C) for 80 minutes. Let rest in pan for 10 minutes before turning out on a rack to cool.

Makes 1 loaf.

Cherry Loaf

A velvety smooth, white pound cake filled with moist maraschino cherries – a must for teas and receptions!

1 cup	butter OR margarine	250 mL
2 cups	white sugar	500 mL
3	eggs	3
1 tsp.	vanilla	5 mL
1 tsp.	lemon flavoring	5 mL
1 tsp.	almond flavoring	5 mL
2 cups	cut maraschino cherries OR glacé cherries	500 mL
3 cups	flour	750 mL
1 tsp.	salt	5 mL
1 tsp.	baking powder	5 mL
¾ cup	warm milk	175 mL

Stop & Snack Awhile

Cherry Loaf

Continued

1. Cream butter and sugar well. Add eggs and flavorings and beat well.
2. Drain maraschino cherries; coat them with ¼ cup (60 mL) of the flour.
3. Combine the remaining flour, salt and baking powder. Add to butter mixture alternately with warm milk, beating well after each addition. Stir the floured cherries into the batter.
4. Spoon the batter into 2 greased 4½ x 8½" (11 x 21 cm) loaf pans. Cover pans with foil and bake for 1½-1¾ hours at 325°F (160°C). (The foil is to prevent the cakes from browning – they remain white on top!) Do not overbake!

Makes 2 small loaves.

Rhubarb Custard Cake

A moist cake with a rhubarb custard filling. Serve it hot or cold.

⅓ cup	butter OR margarine, softened	75 mL
½ cup	brown sugar	125 mL
2 cups	flour	500 mL
1 tsp.	baking powder	5 mL
¼ tsp.	salt	1 mL
1	egg, beaten	1

Rhubarb Filling:

1½ cups	white sugar	375 mL
½ cup	butter OR margarine	125 mL
½ cup	flour	125 mL
2	eggs, well beaten	2
4 cups	diced rhubarb, fresh OR frozen	1 L

Cinnamon Sugar Topping

¼ cup	white sugar	60 mL
1 tsp.	cinnamon	50 mL

1. Combine the butter and sugar and beat with an electric mixer. Add the remaining ingredients to make a crumbly dough. Take out 1 cup (250 mL) and save it for the third layer. Press the remainder into a 9 x 13" (23 x 33 cm) pan.
2. To make filling, beat the sugar and butter with an electric mixer. Add flour and eggs and mix well. Stir in the rhubarb; spread on top of base.
3. Sprinkle reserved crumbs on top of rhubarb mixture.
4. Mix sugar and cinnamon and sprinkle on top of crumbs.
5. Bake at 350°F (160°C) for 45-50 minutes. Cool in the pan.

Makes 12-15 servings.

Orange Lard Cake with Orange Butter Cream Frosting

Well, I know you won't want to use lard, but I have to tell you that this cake isn't the same without it. You won't believe how good it is WITH lard – at least until you try it.

2	eggs, separated	2
½ cup	white sugar	125 mL
2¼ cups	flour	550 mL
1 cup	white sugar	250 mL
2½ tsp.	baking powder	12 mL
1 tsp.	salt	5 mL
¼ tsp.	baking soda	1 mL
⅓ cup	lard, softened	75 mL
¾ cup	milk	175 mL
⅓ cup	orange juice	75 mL
1 tbsp.	freshly grated orange rind	15 mL
¼ tsp.	almond extract	1 mL

1. Beat egg whites until frothy. Gradually beat in ½ cup (125 mL) sugar. Continue beating until stiff and glossy.
2. In another bowl, combine flour, sugar, baking powder, salt and baking soda. Add softened lard and milk. Beat 1 minute. Add orange juice, rind and almond extract. Beat well.
3. Fold egg whites into batter.
4. Bake in a greased 9" (23 cm) square pan at 350°F (180°C) for 25-30 minutes, or until a toothpick inserted in the center comes out clean. Cool in the pan, on a rack. When cool, ice with Orange Butter Cream Frosting.

Makes 1 cake.

Orange Butter Cream Frosting

¼ cup	butter OR margarine	60 mL
1½ cups	icing sugar	375 mL
3 tbsp.	orange juice	45 mL
½ tsp.	grated orange rind	2 mL

1. Cream butter. Gradually add sugar alternately with orange juice. Add orange rind. Beat until light and fluffy.

  *Stop & Snack Awhile*

Taste Teasers

We are more likely to serve an hors d'oeuvre at North Knife Lake than at Dymond Lake. And when we serve one to the hunters at Dymond, it will always be with wild meat or goose. For those treats, you must turn to the Moose, Goose & Things That Swim section of our book. Now, we know that the hungry fishermen at North Knife like to be pampered just a little. So, after a superb day of fishing and a quick shower they come to relax in the large, comfortable lounge where there is an open bar and a choice of Taste Teasers to stave off hunger until the meal is served at 7 p.m. Here are a few of the morsels we have to offer.

Kahlúa or Amaretto Fruit Dip

There is something about sour cream and brown sugar that stimulates the taste buds. Add the liqueur, your favorite fruit and Voilà! – it's magic!

1 cup	sour cream	250 mL
½ cup	brown sugar	125 mL
1 tbsp.	Kahlúa OR amaretto	15 mL

1. Mix all together, chill and serve as a dip with your favorite fresh fruit.

Makes 1½ cups (375 mL) dip

Tangy Orange Fruit Dip

This makes a very large amount, but it does freeze! In fact, when it's frozen, you can serve it like ice cream with fruit on top!

12½ oz.	can frozen orange juice concentrate, thawed	355 mL
10 oz.	can sweetened condensed milk	300 mL
2 x 16 oz.	Cool Whip	2 x 500 mL

1. Mix all together, chill and serve as a dip with your favorite fresh fruit.

Makes 6 cups dip.

"Maggie Goes To Expo"

It was 1986 and we were busy working on the new lodge at North Knife Lake. The old camp is on the north side of a big hill and the new lodge is on the south. I was kneading bread in the old kitchen when all of a sudden, there was a huge explosion. I looked at my helper, Emma, and said, "the lodge has blown up". We went tearing out of the cabin and started up the hill, expecting to see smoke and flames any minute. Well, at the top of the hill, we met up with the plumber and electrician who were running as hard as we were and they wanted to know what had blown up on our side of the hill. They assured us the lodge was fine and we assured them that the kitchen was likewise and, as far as we knew, so were the other cabins. We shook our heads and all went back to work. Everything was quiet for the rest of the weekend, until Monday morning. Emma and I were quietly working when all of a sudden, "BOOM!" There it was again, and I mean it was LOUD, just like it had been on the Friday. Off I went running again. I checked all over but again nothing was out of the ordinary.

Later that week, in Churchill, I checked with the weather office to see if they had any feasible explanation – and this is what I was told. Maggie Thatcher had flown from England to Vancouver to attend Expo that Friday and returned home on Monday. North Knife was on the route that the Concorde flew and we had likely heard it break the sound barrier. Fact or fiction? We don't know but it has never reoccurred!

Taste Teasers

Antipasto

We make our antipasto in rather a large quantity because it keeps so well and is such an easy appetizer to have on hand. I keep a jar in the refrigerator all the time. Any that you won't be using for a month or so just stick in the freezer.

2 cups	finely chopped cauliflower	500 mL
14 oz.	can ripe olives, chopped OR sliced	398 mL
½ cup	chopped green olives	125 mL
1 cup	chopped onion	250 mL
½ cup	vegetable oil	125 mL
10 oz.	can mushrooms, chopped	284 mL
1	finely chopped green pepper	1
1	finely chopped red pepper	1
4½ cups	ketchup	1.125 L
2 cups	sweet relish	500 mL
2 x 6.5 oz.	cans flaked tuna	2 x 184 g
2 x 4.5 oz.	cans broken shrimp	2 x 128 g

1. Put the first 5 ingredients into a very large saucepan. Bring them to a boil and simmer over medium heat for 10 minutes.
2. Add all the rest of the ingredients.
3. Return to a boil and simmer 10 more minutes, stirring often.
4. Pour antipasto into sterilized jars and chill.

This makes 12 cups (3 L).

SERVING SUGGESTION: Place Antipasto in a small bowl in the center of a platter and surround it with assorted crackers or thin slices of hors d'oeuvre bread.

NOTE: Some optional ingredients that can also be added are yellow and green beans, celery and anchovies. Experiment a little. No two batches need be exactly the same!

Shari's Shrimp Spread

It's like a shrimp cocktail served on a cracker!

4 oz.	can small OR broken shrimp	113 g
½ cup	ketchup	125 mL
1 tbsp.	horseradish	15 mL
½ tsp.	celery salt	2 mL
4 drops	Tabasco sauce	4 drops

1. Mix all ingredients together and refrigerate for at least 2 hours. Serve with crackers.

Makes about 1 cup (250 mL) of spread.

Quesadillas

Following the tortillas is a long list of ingredients that can be used in your quesadillas. The recipes given are only suggestions, and the only necessary ingredient is the cheese – it holds it all together.

> large, soft tortillas
> grated Cheddar OR mozzarella cheese
> picante sauce
> salsa
> sour cream
> horseradish
> chopped onion
> chopped sweet peppers, green OR red
> chopped jalapeño peppers
> chopped tomatoes
> sliced mushrooms
> capers
> sliced olives, green OR black
> crumbled bacon
> chopped ham
> any cooked OR smoked meat of your choice
> smoked fish
> anchovies
> refried beans

Warm 1 side of 2 tortillas first on a hot skillet, so that they puff a little (15 seconds will do). Remove tortillas to a working surface, and start building the quesadillas on 1 tortilla, by layering your choice of ingredients. Top with the second tortilla. Return to hot skillet and brown for 1 minute. Turn (that's the challenging part!) and brown on the other side for 1 minute. The cheese should be slightly melted. Remove to a cutting surface, cut into 6 pieces, like a pie, and serve for lunch or snacks*.

See photograph on page 121.

Suggestion #1 – The Starter

> salsa
> crumbled bacon
> chopped onions
> sliced green olives
> grated Cheddar cheese

Suggestion #2 – The Hot One!

sour cream
picante sauce
chopped pepperoni
pickled jalapeño peppers, chopped
sliced black olives
grated mozzarella cheese

Suggestion #3 – North Knife Lake Special

sour cream
horseradish
chopped tomatoes
smoked fish
capers
sliced black olives
grated Cheddar and mozzarella cheeses

This is finger food, like a sandwich. Generally make 1 double quesadilla per person.

* To serve as an hors d'oeuvre, cut each slice into irregular shapes. Decorate with slices of jalapeño or olive, held in place with a toothpick.

Olive Lover's Cheese Ball

(MARIE) This has been a favorite at our house for many years, and it simply evolved from my family's passion for green olives.

8 oz.	cream cheese, softened	250 g
1	large garlic clove, crushed	1
½ cup	finely chopped celery	125 mL
½ cup	chopped green onions	125 mL
½ cup	finely chopped green pepper	125 mL
½ cup	chopped stuffed green olives	125 mL
2 cups	grated Cheddar cheese	500 mL

Mix all together. Form into a ball or place in a bowl. Serve with crackers.

Makes 1 cheese ball.

Mexican Antipasto

8 oz.	cream cheese, softened	250 g
1	garlic clove, crushed	1
½ cup	sour cream	125 mL
1	large avocado, mashed	1
¼ tsp.	lemon juice	1 mL
1	tomato, finely chopped	1
4 oz.	can green chilies*, finely chopped	114 mL
5	slices bacon, fried crisp and crumbled	5
4	stuffed green olives, sliced	4
¼ cup	black olives, sliced	60 mL
1 cup	taco sauce, hot, medium OR mild	250 mL
1 cup	grated Cheddar cheese	250 mL

1. Combine the cream cheese, garlic and sour cream. Spread in a 9" (23 cm) pie plate.
2. Combine the mashed avocado, lemon juice, tomato and chilies. Spread over the cheese mixture.
3. Sprinkle with the bacon and olives. Spread taco sauce over all. Top with grated Cheddar.

Serves 12.

SERVING SUGGESTION: Serve with corn chips, taco chips or crackers.

* *For more of a bite, add finely chopped jalapeño peppers to green chilies.*

Crab Cheese Puffs

Crabby, puffy and square – also classy and delicious. Try them!

14 oz.	pkg. puff pastry	397 g
1½ cups	shredded Swiss OR Monterey Jack cheese	375 mL
2 cups	chopped crab	500 mL
½ cup	salad dressing	125 mL
3 cups	chopped green onion (yes, it's a lot!)	750 mL
dash	Tabasco	dash
1	sweet red pepper, thinly sliced	1

1. Following the directions on the package, roll out enough pastry to fit a greased cookie sheet (with raised sides).
2. Combine cheese, crab, salad dressing, onion and Tabasco, and spread on puff pastry. Cover with slices of red pepper.
3. Bake at 400°F (200°C) for 15-20 minutes. Cut into squares and serve.

Serves 12-16.

NOTE: Do not spread crab mixture on pastry until you are ready to bake it, as it will become soggy.

Taste Teasers

Crab-Stuffed Mushroom Caps

(MARIE) From a visit to Branson, Missouri, where our son, Todd, plays in the Country Tonite Theatre, comes this wonderful appetizer.

30	large mushrooms	30
½ cup	butter OR margarine	125 mL
8 oz.	cream cheese, softened	250 g
6 oz.	crab meat	170 g
1 tbsp.	minced onion	15 mL
8 drops	Tabasco sauce	8 drops
1 tsp.	salt	5 mL
1 tsp.	pepper	5 mL
1 tbsp.	Worcestershire sauce	15 mL

1. Wash mushrooms and remove stems. Place caps in a baking pan, and brush with melted butter.
2. Meanwhile, combine cream cheese and crab meat with remaining ingredients. Place 1 heaping tsp. (7 mL) of crab mixture in each mushroom cap. Bake at 350°F (180°C) for 10-15 minutes.

SERVING SUGGESTION: Spread any leftover crab mixture on crackers.

Makes 30 caps.

Honey-Mustard Chicken Bites

A little spicy, a little hot, a whole lot of tasty!

1 lb.	boned, skinless chicken breasts	500 g

Honey Mustard Marinade or Sauce:

⅓ cup	spicy brown mustard	75 mL
3 tbsp.	honey	45 mL
2 tbsp.	ketchup	30 mL
1	garlic clove, minced	1
½ tsp.	Tabasco sauce	2 mL

1. Cut the chicken into 1" (2.5 cm) pieces.
2. Mix marinade ingredients in a bowl. Set aside ¼ cup (60 mL) to use as a sauce. Add the chicken to the marinade; stir to coat. Cover and refrigerate for at least 1 hour, stirring occasionally.
3. Preheat broiler. Arrange chicken pieces on a rack in the broiler pan and broil, turning once and brushing with marinade until chicken is tender, about 10 minutes. Serve with reserved sauce as a dip.

Serves 6.

Louisiana Hot Wings – Screamin' or Whimperin'

These oven-baked wings give you half the grease and all the flavor!

3 lbs.	chicken wings	1.5 kg
1 cup	flour	250 mL
1 tsp.	DLS* OR ½ tsp. (2 mL) salt and ½ tsp. (2 mL) pepper	5 mL
3	eggs, beaten	3
	Louisiana hot sauce	
	sour cream	

1. Cut off the wing tips and discard or freeze for another use. Cut remaining wings in 2 pieces. (You will now have 1 piece that looks like a tiny drumstick and 1 piece that still looks like a wing – sort of.)
2. Mix the flour with DLS* in a small, shallow pan.
3. Dip the wings in beaten egg, then roll in flour mixture.
4. Place the wings on a well-oiled baking sheet and bake at 400°F (200°C) for ½ hour, or until well browned.
5. Remove the wings to a large shallow casserole or baking pan.
6. Turn the oven down to 350°F (180°C).
7. For SCREAMIN' wings, brush both sides of wings liberally with Louisiana hot sauce. Return wings to oven and bake for 15-20 minutes.
8. For WHIMPERIN' wings, mix some Louisiana hot sauce with sour cream. Brush mixture on wings and bake at 350°F (180°C) for 15-20 minutes. You'll have to experiment with amounts to see how you like it!

Serves 12 as appetizers or 6 for dinner.

* *Dymond Lake Seasoning*

See photograph on page 121.

A Boating Fable

Once upon a time a great king had a heavy throne. He also had a little boat. He liked to go out in his boat sitting on his throne. One day, while he enjoyed the boat and the water, a sudden breeze sprang up and rocked the little boat. The heavy throne slid to one side of the boat. The little boat toppled over, causing the king to lose a lot of things, not the least of which was his dignity.

MORAL: People with small boats shouldn't stow thrones!

  Taste Teasers

Simply Salad

*Pasta salads, jellies, fresh fruit and vegetable salads –
some are a meal in themselves, and some are a great
accompaniment to a meal. Our absolute favorites in this
section are Egyptian Salad from Betty, Helen's friend, and
Minted Green Bean Salad from Jane, Marie's sister. We
hope they will forgive us for taking some liberties with
the originals. We think that these salads are unique and
uniquely irresistible.*

Tomatoes Vinaigrette

These tomatoes may be made ahead, or the marinade may be used as a dressing at the time of serving. Either way, you have a very tasty and simple salad.

4	large tomatoes, sliced thickly	4
¼ cup	chopped green onion OR sliced red onion	60 mL

Herbed Wine Vinegar Marinade:

1 cup	olive oil	250 mL
⅓ cup	wine vinegar	75 mL
2 tsp.	dried oregano OR 2 tbsp. (30 mL) chopped fresh	10 mL
½ tsp.	salt	2 mL
1 tsp.	DLS* or seasoned pepper	5 mL
½ tsp.	dry mustard powder	2 mL
2	garlic cloves, crushed	2
1 tbsp.	chopped parsley, or parsley flakes	15 mL

1. Put the tomatoes and onions in a flat dish.
2. Mix the marinade and pour over. Marinate up to 4 hours OR serve immediately. Serve on a bed of lettuce leaves or on its own.

Serves 6-8.

* *Dymond Lake Seasoning*

Vanity, Thy Name is Helen

(HELEN) Doug called home from work one day and suggested a weekend with friends, Bob and Maggie Fortin, in a nice little trapper's cabin in the bush. I was assured that this cosy wee cabin had all the necessities like beds, a heater and cook-stove, and with our big down sleeping bags we would be as snug as hibernating bears. Well, it sounded like a pleasant adventure so I arranged for a sitter, planned our menu and did some packing. Early Saturday we set off. The sun was shining; it was only -20°F – a truly balmy Churchill day. By midafternoon we made it to the cabin which was nestled into a big snowbank and looked very quaint. The men shoveled out the door and in we went. There were beds all right – spruce trees hammered together to make frames, with spruce boughs laid over them for mattresses. And the heater and cookstove? – they were combined in one, 10-gallon drum cut in half with a lid welded on. Cooking dinner was a major undertaking. Maggie and I fed paper into the stove under the frying pan; that was the only way we could get enough flames going to sizzle the hamburgers. Now it was time to get into those comfy beds – but not without putting my hair in rollers! Bob could not believe that I had actually brought them 25 miles into the bush. But the real laugh for him was the next morning when I took them out, combed my hair and tried to spray it – my hairspray was frozen in the can! That was over 25 years ago and Bob still likes to tell this story!

(MARIE) Helen has been blessed with wonderful, naturally curly hair. But you still won't catch her without her blow-dryer and hairspray "in the middle of the bush!" She's a classy lady!

Tomato and Cucumber Salad with Feta Cheese

A very easy, tangy salad, with a tart vinegar flavor. We like to sop up the dressing with French bread – to lick the bowl clean!

1	large tomato, quartered and thinly sliced	1
½	medium cucumber, peeled, quartered and thinly sliced	½
½ cup	quartered, thinly sliced red onion	125 mL
⅔ cup	crumbled feta cheese	150 mL
¼ cup	olive oil	60 mL
¼ cup	red wine vinegar	60 mL
½ tsp.	dried crumbled marjoram, OR 1 tbsp. (15 mL) fresh	2 mL
½ tsp.	salt	2 mL

1. Place the sliced tomato, cucumber and onion in a small salad bowl. Add the feta cheese.
2. In another small bowl, combine the olive oil, wine vinegar, marjoram and salt. Pour over the vegetables.
3. Mix well and let the salad stand at least an hour before serving.

Serves 4.

Egyptian Salad

If you are a lover of feta cheese, this will come as an absolute delight. The saltiness of feta mingled with the sweetness of fruit sets the taste buds dancing at the mere thought!

8 cups	torn Romaine lettuce	2 L
½ cup	crumbled feta cheese	125 mL
1 cup	seedless grapes, red and/or green	250 mL
¼ cup	thinly sliced red OR sweet onions (optional)	60 mL

Lemon Dressing:

¼ cup	olive oil	60 mL
2 tbsp.	lemon juice	30 mL
1 tsp.	sugar	5 mL
	pepper (optional)	

1. Prepare salad ingredients and combine in a large bowl.
2. Mix dressing ingredients and toss with salad ingredients, just before serving.

Serves 6.

Minted Green Bean Salad

(MARIE) My sister has been making a version of this salad for years, and I've been enjoying it for just as long. She loves vinegar; I prefer to soften the vinegar taste with mayonnaise, so that's how I've written the recipe. I know that you will enjoy the crisp freshness of this salad, so be sure to try it when fresh beans are in season.

Salad:

(Amounts given are a guideline and not meant to be exact)

1-2 cups	fresh green beans in 2" (5 cm) pieces	250-500 mL
1 cup	sliced fresh mushrooms	250 mL
½	small red onion, sliced thinly	½
6-8 cups	torn romaine lettuce	1.5-2 L
	a few fresh mint leaves (optional)	

Mint Dressing:

½ cup	mint vinegar*	125 mL
2 tbsp.	olive oil	30 mL
2 tbsp.	dried basil OR ⅔ cup (150 mL) chopped fresh	30 mL
1 tbsp.	white sugar	15 mL
1 tsp.	salt	5 mL
½ cup	mayonnaise	125 mL

1. Mix together the salad ingredients.
2. In a jar, mix together all the dressing ingredients.
3. Just before serving, add the dressing gradually to the lettuce mixture – you may not need the full amount. Store the leftover dressing in a jar in the refrigerator.

Serves 6-8.

* *To make mint vinegar, fill a small jar with fresh mint leaves. Pour white vinegar over them to fill the jar. Let sit for a few hours. If fresh mint leaves are not available, replace the mint vinegar in the recipe with bottled mint sauce. At North Knife Lake Lodge we can pick wild mint just outside the kitchen door.*

Taste Teasers – Wild & Tame

Landlocked Lobster, page 30
Quesadillas, page 112
Venison Hot Shots, page 8
Pizza Bread with Cheese, page 57
Louisiana Hot Wings, page 116
Duck Liver Pâté, page 16

  Simply Salad

Greek Pasta Salad

If you enjoy our regular Greek Salad (Blueberries & Polar Bears, page 114) you will want to try our Greek Pasta Salad too. Tastes even better the second day.

Greek Dressing:

½ cup	olive oil	125 mL
¼ cup	red wine vinegar	60 mL
2	small garlic cloves, crushed	2
½ tsp.	dried oregano OR 1 tbsp. (15 mL) chopped fresh	2 mL
½ tsp.	dried basil OR 1 tbsp. (15 mL) chopped fresh	2 mL
½ tsp.	salt	2 mL
¼ tsp.	pepper	1 mL

Pasta Salad:

4 cups	cooked macaroni (2 cups [500 mL] uncooked)	1 L
1 cup	chopped tomatoes	250 mL
1 cup	chopped cucumber	250 mL
½ cup	chopped green pepper	125 mL
¼ cup	chopped red onion	60 mL
½ cup	sliced black olives	125 mL
½ cup	crumbled feta cheese	125 mL
½ cup	Greek dressing (above)	125 mL
	freshly ground black pepper	

1. Combine all dressing ingredients.
2. In a large bowl, combine all salad ingredients. Add dressing and toss well. Top with freshly ground black pepper or a coarse seasoned pepper. This salad tastes better if you make it ahead and refrigerate it for a couple of hours. This gives the flavors time to blend.

Serves 6-8.

Canada Geese at Dymond Lake.

Neptune Pasta Salad

Serve this simple flavorful lunch salad with fresh vegetables, cold cuts and buns.

3 cups	raw shell pasta (4½ cups [1.125 L] cooked)	750 mL
6 oz.	can chunk tuna, drained, broken up	170 g
¼ cup	chopped onion	60 mL
¼ cup	chopped red pepper	60 mL
¼ cup	chopped green pepper	60 mL
½ cup	chopped cucumber	125 mL
¾ cup	mayonnaise OR salad dressing	175 mL
½ cup	sour cream	125 mL
1 tbsp.	vinegar	15 mL
½ tsp.	salt	2 mL
½ tsp.	pepper	2 mL

1. Cook pasta in salted water until tender. Drain, rinse in cold water and drain again. Add tuna and chopped vegetables.
2. Mix mayonnaise with sour cream, vinegar, salt and pepper. Pour over salad and mix well. Cover and chill until ready to serve.

Makes 6 cups (1.5 L) to serve 6-8.

NOTE: This tastes even better the second day, but it may need a little more dressing as the pasta tends to absorb it.

Mandarin Rice Salad

A weekend camping trip turned up this recipe. It is great to put in your lunch, take to a potluck or as an addition to a cold summer meal. This salad keeps in the refrigerator for a week.

2 cups	water	500 mL
1 tsp.	salt	5 mL
1 cup	raw rice, brown OR white (not instant)	250 mL
1½ cups	sliced OR button mushrooms OR 10 oz. (284 mL) can	375 mL
4 tbsp.	soy sauce	60 mL
½ cup	vinegar	125 mL
⅓ cup	vegetable oil	75 mL
1 cup	chopped celery	250 mL
2 tbsp.	chopped green onion	30 mL
10 oz.	can mandarin oranges, drained	284 mL
½ cup	slivered OR sliced almonds	125 mL

  *Simply Salad*

Mandarin Rice Salad

Continued

1. Bring the water to a boil in a heavy saucepan; add salt and rice. Reduce heat and simmer for 20 minutes, 40 minutes for brown rice. Cool completely before proceeding.
2. Marinate rice with mushrooms in the soy sauce, vinegar and oil. Cover and let sit in refrigerator overnight.
3. Add chopped celery and green onion. Mix well. Place in a bowl or casserole and garnish with mandarin oranges and almonds.

Serves 6.

Waldorf Salad

One day a friend called to see if I had a recipe for Waldorf Salad. I couldn't find a recipe anywhere. This summer, Myrtle, who worked with us at North Knife Lake Lodge, whipped this up out of her head. We fell in love with it, so here it is, Heather!

1	apple, cut into bite-sized pieces	1
1 cup	seedless green grapes	250 mL
2 cups	sliced celery	500 mL
½ cup	very coarsely chopped pecans	125 mL
½ cup	mayonnaise	125 mL
1 tsp.	white sugar	5 mL

1. Mix all together. Chill for several hours. Serve on lettuce or as is.

Serves 6.

Simply Delicious Apple Coleslaw

From Sue, in the Peace River country of Northern Alberta, comes this tasty salad. You just have to try it!

2	Granny Smith apples, grated	2
2 cups	grated red cabbage	500 mL
1 cup	peeled, grated carrot	250 mL
	mayonnaise to taste	

1. Mix all together, and serve. Mmmmmmm!

Serves 6.

 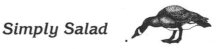

24-Hour Fruit Salad

What the name is trying to tell you is that you have to make this one day ahead. It will also keep for a few days, so don't worry about leftovers.

2	eggs, beaten	2
¼ cup	white sugar	60 mL
¼ cup	white vinegar	60 mL
2 tbsp.	butter OR margarine	30 mL
1 cup	whipping cream	125 mL
8 cups	fresh fruit*, cut into bite-sized pieces, drained if necessary	2 L

1. In a small saucepan, mix eggs, sugar, vinegar and butter until well blended. Cook over low heat, stirring constantly, until smooth and thickened. Let cool.
2. Whip the cream until thick and add to cooled sauce.
3. Stir in fruit. Put in a serving bowl, cover and refrigerate overnight.

Serves 10-12.

* *Apples, oranges, bananas, pears, peaches, grapes, strawberries, kiwi.*

Triple Orange Salad

The rich, tangy orange flavor of this salad complements cold meats on a hot day. It is especially good with ham.

10 oz.	can mandarin oranges	284 mL
	water	
3 oz.	pkg. orange gelatin	85 g
6 oz.	can frozen orange juice concentrate OR	115 mL
	1 cup (250 mL) orange sherbet*	

1. Drain the juice from the mandarin oranges into a measuring cup. Add water to make 1 cup (250 mL). Set oranges aside.
2. Heat the orange liquid in a small saucepan. As soon as it starts to boil, pour it over the orange gelatin in a bowl. Stir well to dissolve.
3. Add the frozen orange juice concentrate to the gelatin and stir well to melt the orange juice. Refrigerate until it begins to set, about 1 hour.
4. Stir in oranges. Return to refrigerator and allow to set completely.

Makes 3 cups (750 mL). Serves 6.

SERVING SUGGESTION: This salad can also be made in a mold.

* *Sherbet gives a creamier consistency than orange concentrate.*

Pineapple Cheese Mold

This dish is served at the lodge for special occasions such as Canada Day or July 4th. We usually do a big buffet with turkey and cranberry sauce, ham, potato salad, marinated vegetables, coleslaw, fresh rolls and of course Pineapple Cheese Mold.

3 oz.	pkg. lime gelatin	85 g
1 cup	boiling water	250 mL
1 cup	half and half cream OR evaporated milk	250 mL
8 oz.	cream cheese, softened	250 g
14 oz.	can crushed pineapple, drained	398 mL
½ cup	mayonnaise	125 mL
¼ cup	chopped celery	60 mL
¼ cup	chopped walnuts OR pecans	60 mL

1. Dissolve the gelatin in boiling water. Stir well to dissolve completely.
2. Add the cream and cream cheese; beat with electric mixer or wire whisk until smooth.
3. Stir in the rest of the ingredients and pour into a clear glass bowl or a mold.
4. Place in the refrigerator and chill until firmly set.

Serves 12.

Blue Cheese Dressing or Dip – In the Pink

1 cup	mayonnaise OR salad dressing	250 mL
½ tsp.	Worcestershire sauce	2 mL
2 tsp.	sugar	10 mL
2 tsp.	lemon juice	10 mL
¼ cup	ketchup	60 mL
⅓ cup	crumbled blue cheese	75 mL

1. Combine all the ingredients and serve as a vegetable dip or salad dressing.

Makes about 1½ cups (375 mL).

VARIATION: For a traditional Blue Cheese dressing, omit the ketchup and blend in a blender.

NOTE: This tends to get runny if it is kept for too long.

Festive Cranberry Mold

For the festive season, or a special cold salad, try this cheerful mold.

3 oz.	pkg. raspberry gelatin	85g
3 oz.	pkg. lemon gelatin	85g
½ cup	white sugar	125 mL
3 cups	boiling water	750 mL
1 tbsp.	lemon juice	15 mL
8¾ oz.	can crushed pineapple	250 mL
2 cups	fresh cranberries	500 mL
1	small orange	1
1 cup	diced celery	250 mL
½ cup	chopped pecans	125 mL

1. Dissolve the gelatins and sugar in boiling water.
2. Mix in lemon juice and undrained crushed pineapple. Chill until partially set, about 1½ hours.
3. Chop or grind cranberries. Peel orange and remove seeds. Chop or grind orange in a blender.
4. Add cranberries, oranges, celery and pecans to partially set gelatin. Pour into an 8½-cup (2 L) mold; chill until firm, 12 hours or more.

Serves 12 or more.

Creamy DLS* Dressing

Yes, you need Dymond Lake Seasoning to make this dressing authentic but you can experiment with other spice mixtures, OR try the spices listed below.

1 cup	olive oil	250 mL
⅓ cup	red wine vinegar	75 mL
2 tsp.	DLS*	10 mL
½ tsp.	salt	2 mL
1 tbsp.	sugar	15 mL
2	garlic cloves, crushed	2
½ cup	mayonnaise OR salad dressing	125 mL

1. Combine all ingredients and mix well.

Makes approximately 2 cups (500 mL) dressing.

* *For Dymond Lake Seasoning, substitute ½ tsp. (2 mL) each thyme, basil, oregano, marjoram and seasoned pepper. Increase salt to 1 tsp.(5 mL).*

  Simply Salad

Vegging Out

Serving a good variety of vegetable dishes is probably our biggest challenge at the camps. Guests are often with us for a week, and we really don't want to duplicate any part of a meal. Now, how often do you have seven different fresh vegetables on hand? We can't usually get that great a variety either – given the fact that groceries probably arrive only once a week. So, we're happy when we find a good recipe for using frozen vegetables, such as Sudden Valley Green Beans or Creamed or Curried Corn; or a new combination of vegetables, as in Cauliflower and Tomato Scallop or Creamy Tomato and Onion Surprise. Our Sweet and Sour Baked Beans, made from all canned ingredients, is a casserole second to none, and can be frozen and reheated without losing any of its great flavor. Whether you have fresh, frozen or canned vegetables on hand, we've got something tasty for you!

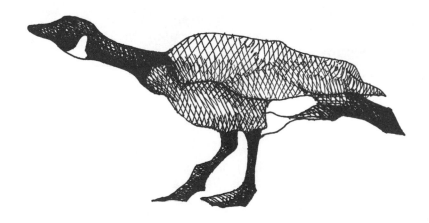

Garlicky Fried Rice 'N' Peas (Or Beans)

In some varieties, the names peas and beans seem to be interchangeable – hence the name of the recipe. They may also be called legumes. Rice and legumes are a delicious combination, very common in many countries of the world. This one is nicely spiced with garlic and red pepper. Other vegetables may also be added.

1 cup	long-grain rice	250 mL
2 cups	chicken stock	500 mL
1 tsp.	salt	5 mL
¼ tsp.	crushed red chili pepper (or equivalent)	1 mL
1-2	garlic cloves, crushed	1-2
1 cup	onion, chopped	250 mL
½ cup	chopped green pepper	125 mL
2 tbsp.	olive oil	30 mL
¼ tsp.	seasoned pepper	1 mL
19 oz.	can kidney beans, drained*	540 mL

1. Measure rice, stock, salt and red pepper into saucepan. Bring to a boil, cover and simmer for 20 minutes, or until rice is cooked.
2. Sauté the garlic, onions and green pepper in olive oil. When the onions are translucent, add seasoned pepper and kidney beans. Heat until beans are warm.
3. Mix the bean mixture with the rice. Serve immediately, or place in a casserole and keep warm in the oven until ready to serve.

Serves 6-8.

* *Many varieties of canned beans or peas are available. Try pigeon beans or black-eyed peas, chickpeas (garbanzo beans). OR, if you are doubling the recipe, try a mixture of beans and peas.*

Paul had been out fishing all day with no luck. On his way home he stopped at Cimolis' fish market. He said to the owner, "Just stand over there and throw me five of your biggest trout." "Throw 'em?" asked Cimoli. "What for?" "So" explained Paul, "I can tell my wife I caught 'em. I may be a poor fisherman, but I'm no liar."

  Vegging Out

Saffron Rice

This is a good rice dish to accompany fish, chicken or any meat that isn't cooked with a sauce.

1 cup	chopped onion	250 mL
1	garlic clove, minced	1
2 tbsp.	olive oil	30 mL
1 cup	rice	250 mL
2 cups	chicken broth	500 mL
1-2 tsp.	saffron	5-10 mL
1 tsp.	salt	5 mL
1 tsp.	whole peppercorns	5 mL
¼ cup	pine nuts (optional)	60 mL

1. In a medium saucepan, over medium heat, sauté the onion and garlic in olive oil until the onion is translucent. Add the raw rice and stir until rice is well covered with oil.
2. Add the chicken broth, saffron, salt and peppercorns. Bring to a boil, cover and simmer for 20 minutes, or until rice is tender, adding more water if necessary. Add pine nuts and season with more pepper, if desired.

Serves 6.

Crispy Round Oven Fries

This is a great way to satisfy your family's (or guest's) craving for French fries with a fraction of the calories, a fraction of the work and no greasy-spoon smell.

6	large potatoes, peeled OR unpeeled depending on the condition of their skin	6
3 tbsp.	vegetable oil	45 mL
	salt OR seasoned salt*	

1. Preheat the oven to 450°F (230°C). Spray baking sheets lightly with a nonstick cooking spray.
2. Slice the potatoes into ¼" (6 mm) rounds. Toss in a bowl with the oil and spread on baking sheets. Sprinkle with salt or seasoned salt.
3. Bake for 20 minutes, turning once after 10 minutes.

Serves 4-6.

* Dymond Lake Seasoning may be added, if desired.

COOKING TIP: To release the starch in the sliced potatoes, soak them in cold water for 2 hours. Drain potatoes and pat them dry before tossing with oil.

See photograph on page 69.

Baked Potato – What A Slice!

Easier than stuffed potatoes, and just as impressive. Amounts given are just a guide. Go ahead and make as many as you need!

4	potatoes	4
2-3 tbsp.	butter OR margarine, melted	30-45 mL
1 tsp.	salt	5 mL
2-3 tbsp.	chopped combined fresh herbs OR 2-3 tsp. (10-15 mL) dried (parsley, chives, thyme OR sage)	30-45 mL
4 tbsp.	grated Cheddar cheese	60 mL
2 tsp.	grated Parmesan cheese	10 mL

1. Scrub potatoes and slice them every ¼" (6 mm), but not all the way through. Fan out potatoes and place them in a baking dish.
2. Brush butter between each slice. Mix together the herbs and salt and sprinkle between each slice.
3. Bake potatoes, uncovered, at 425°F (220°C) for 50 minutes. Remove them from the oven, sprinkle with cheeses and bake for 10 minutes.

Serves 4.

Paprika Potatoes

These differ from other oven-baked potatoes in the flavor and color of the paprika. They make an attractive presentation.

½ cup	butter OR margarine	125 mL
¼ cup	flour	60 mL
¼ cup	Parmesan cheese	60 mL
1 tbsp.	paprika	15 mL
¾ tsp.	salt	3 mL
⅛ tsp.	pepper	0.5 mL
⅛ tsp.	garlic powder	0.5 mL
6	medium potatoes, quartered lengthwise (peeled OR unpeeled)	6

1. Melt butter in a 9 x 13" (23 x 33 cm) baking pan. Combine the dry ingredients. Be sure potatoes are damp, then shake them, a few at a time, in the dry ingredients to coat well. The more of the spice mixture that adheres to the potatoes the better they will taste. Place potatoes in a single layer in the baking pan.
2. Bake, uncovered, at 350°F (180°C) for 50-60 minutes, turning once after 30 minutes.

Serves 4-6.

Vegging Out

Garlicky Mashed Potatoes

Baked garlic is becoming very popular. When baked, it has a milder flavor and, when teamed with onion and potatoes, garlic gives a flavorful twist to the old stand-by, mashed potatoes.

1	whole head of garlic, unpeeled	1
1	large white onion, peeled	1
1 tbsp.	olive oil OR butter	15 mL
6	large potatoes	6
6 tbsp.	butter	90 mL
	milk	
	salt and freshly ground pepper	

1. ***Baked Garlic and Onion:*** Preheat oven to 450°F (230°C). Place the garlic head and onion on a square of aluminum foil large enough to completely enclose them. Drizzle the olive oil over garlic and onion. Seal the aluminum foil around them and roast in the oven for 45 minutes. Carefully unwrap the foil, and test garlic and onion to be sure they are soft. Bake a little longer, if necessary. Let them cool slightly.
2. Cut the onion into smaller pieces and place in a food processor. Squeeze the garlic out of the unpeeled cloves into the food processor with the onion and purée.
3. Peel the potatoes and cut into chunks. Boil in salted water for 20 minutes, or until soft. Drain potatoes and discard the water.
4. Mash the potatoes with the garlic/onion purée. Beat with a mixer, if desired. Add the butter. Add milk cautiously, for a smoother consistency. Add salt and freshly ground pepper to taste.

Serves 6.

SERVING SUGGESTION: *Sprinkle with paprika, chives, or Dymond Lake Seasoning. These potatoes are also good with gravy.*

NOTE: *Baked garlic is great on crusty French bread with a hearty soup.*

See photograph on page 155.

Goose Facts – What's For Dinner?

Canada geese feed on tender grasses and grains, water plants and tundra berries, depending on their location. Newborn goslings gain about a pound per week to reach six or seven pounds in two months.

Sweet Squash

There is a large variety of squash on the market in the fall. Butternut, buttercup, acorn and hubbard are the most common. This fancy vegetable dish would definitely complement a roast chicken and mashed potato dinner.

6 cups	cooked, mashed squash	1.5 L
¼ cup	butter OR margarine, melted	60 mL
½ cup	grated onion	125 mL
2	eggs, beaten	2
2 tbsp.	brown sugar	30 mL
½ tsp.	salt	2 mL
½ tsp.	pepper OR DLS*	2 mL
2 cups	seasoned croûtons, crushed, OR 1 cup (250 mL) dry bread crumbs	500 mL
½ cup	butter OR margarine, melted	125 mL

1. Peel squash, remove seeds and cut in large chunks. Cook in a small amount of water until tender. Discard water and mash squash. (6 cups [1.5 L] is approximate and is to be used as a guide only.)
2. Combine the squash with ¼ cup (60 mL) butter, onion, eggs, brown sugar, salt and pepper. Place in a 2-quart (2 L) casserole, and bake at 350°F (180°C) for 30 minutes.
3. Combine crushed croûtons with melted butter and sprinkle over casserole. Bake another 30 minutes.

Serves 6-8.

VARIATION: Sweet potato may be used instead of squash. Boil the potatoes in their skins in water to cover until tender, about 25 minutes. Cool a little; peel potatoes and mash, then continue with step 2.

* *Dymond Lake Seasoning*

Max and Moe went out ice-fishing one day. Max drilled a hole in the ice and, to his great surprise, heard a voice calling, "There are no fish here!" Thinking he must indeed have a direct line to the Almighty, he moved, drilled another hole and heard the same voice again "There are no fish here!" A third time he moved and drilled, and again heard the voice, "This is the arena manager, there are no fish here!"

Cheesy Squash Casserole

Squash is a vegetable that it seems we have to acquire a taste for. Personally, I love it – but if you want to try a dressed up version on those not yet converted – this is it!

1	squash* (butternut, hubbard OR acorn)	1
	salted water	
	butter	
	pepper OR cayenne to taste	
¼ cup	butter	60 mL
½ cup	chopped onion	125 mL
½ cup	chopped celery	125 mL
1½ cups	sliced fresh mushrooms OR 10 oz. (284 mL) can, drained	375 mL
½ tsp.	salt	2 mL
⅛ tsp.	pepper	0.5 mL
2 tbsp.	chopped parsley	30 mL
1 cup	grated Cheddar cheese	250 mL

1. Peel the squash, discard seeds and cut flesh into chunks. Simmer squash in a small amount of salted water, until tender, about 10 minutes. Drain, mash and season squash with butter and pepper to taste. Place squash in a buttered 9" (23 cm) square casserole.
2. In a small frying pan, cook the onion and celery in ¼ cup (60 mL) butter until onions are translucent, about 10 minutes. Add mushrooms and cook 2-3 minutes more. Add salt, pepper and parsley. Spread the onion mixture evenly over the squash. Cover and bake 15 minutes.
3. Remove cover, distribute grated cheese evenly over vegetables. Return to oven and bake 5 minutes more, uncovered.

Serves 6.

* *The type of squash used will determine how many you need. The amount isn't critical. 4-6 cups (1-1.5 L) of mashed squash is good. An alternate method may be used with acorn squash. Take 3 medium squash, cut them in half and remove the seeds. Bake squash, covered, in a small amount of water at 350°F (180°C) until almost tender, about 45 minutes. Discard water and proceed with step 2.*

Sweet and Sour Baked Beans

I have it on good authority that the baking takes the "toot" out of the beans! These are good enough for company and they freeze well.

19 oz.	can garbanzo beans* (chickpeas), drained	540 mL
14 oz.	EACH can red kidney and lima beans*, drained	398 mL
28 oz.	can Boston baked beans	796 mL
8	bacon slices	8
2	large onions, sliced OR chopped	2
1	garlic clove, crushed	1
1 cup	brown sugar	250 mL
1 tsp.	dry mustard	5 mL
1 tsp.	salt	5 mL
½ cup	vinegar	125 mL

1. Combine the beans in a 4-quart (4 L) ovenproof casserole or pan. (Don't forget to drain all but the Boston beans.)
2. Fry the bacon until crisp. Crumble bacon into the beans. Reserve 2 tbsp. (30 mL) bacon fat in the pan and discard the rest.
3. Sauté the onions and garlic in the bacon fat over medium heat until onions are translucent. Add brown sugar, mustard, salt and vinegar. Heat to boiling. Add to the beans in the casserole.
4. Bake at 350°F (180°C) for 1 hour, or until bubbly.

Serves 10-12.

* *Any similar beans may be substituted except for the Boston baked beans.*

See photograph on page 17.

Nifty Carrots

5-6	carrots	5-6
¼ cup	carrot water	60 mL
¼ cup	EACH mayonnaise and sour cream	60 mL
2 tbsp.	finely chopped onion	30 mL
1 tbsp.	horseradish	15 mL
	salt and pepper, to taste	
1 tbsp.	butter OR margarine, melted	15 mL
½ cup	dried bread crumbs	125 mL

1. Slice carrots and cook them in a little water, until tender-crisp, about 10 minutes. Place the carrots in a shallow casserole.
2. Combine the water, mayonnaise, sour cream, onion, horseradish, salt and pepper and pour over the carrots.
3. Combine melted butter and bread crumbs and sprinkle over casserole. Bake at 350°F (180°C) for 30 minutes.

Serves 6.

Vegging Out

Sudden Valley Green Beans

Once in a while you are caught without fresh vegetables on hand. It happens! Try this tasty version of an old standby!

Mushroom Sauce*:

¼ cup	butter OR margarine	60 mL
½ cup	chopped mushrooms	125 mL
¼ cup	chopped onion	60 mL
1	small garlic clove, crushed	1
2 tbsp.	flour	30 mL
¼ tsp.	salt	1 mL
⅛ tsp.	pepper	0.5 mL
1 cup	milk	250 mL
½ cup	chicken stock	125 mL
10 oz.	pkg. French-style, frozen green beans	283 g
1½ cups	sliced fresh mushrooms OR 10 oz. (284 mL) can, drained	375 mL
2 tbsp.	butter OR margarine	30 mL
½ cup	croûtons	125 mL
⅓ cup	Parmesan cheese	75 mL

1. Melt butter in saucepan; add mushrooms, onion and garlic; sauté until onions are translucent. Add flour and stir until smooth. Add milk, gradually, whisking to keep smooth. Add chicken stock. Cook and whisk until thickened.
2. Layer beans and mushrooms in a 1-quart (1 L) casserole.
3. Pour Mushroom Sauce over vegetables in casserole.
4. Melt butter in a small saucepan. Add the croûtons and stir to coat them with the butter. Sprinkle croûtons over casserole. Sprinkle with cheese.
5. Bake, uncovered, at 350°F (180°C) for 50-60 minutes.

Serves 6.

* *If you are in a hurry, 1 can (10 oz. [284 mL]) mushroom soup and ⅓ cup (75 mL) milk makes a convenient and quick alternative to Mushroom Sauce.*

Creamed or Curried Corn

Our staff and guests at the lodges have thoroughly enjoyed our homemade creamed corn – the flavor is much smoother and richer than the canned variety.

Creamed Corn

3 tbsp.	butter OR margarine	45 mL
3 tbsp.	flour	45 mL
1 cup	milk	250 mL
4 cups	kernel corn, canned OR frozen	1 L
	salt and pepper	

1. Over medium heat, melt the butter in a saucepan. Add the flour. Stir until the butter is absorbed. Gradually add the milk, stirring constantly while the mixture thickens. Use a whisk, if necessary, to keep it smooth. Stir in corn, salt and pepper. Cover, reduce heat, and simmer until hot.

Serves 3-4.

VARIATION: CURRIED CORN: Add 1 tsp. (5 mL) curry powder with the flour; add 2 sliced green onions with the corn.

NOTE: These recipes are also very good made with carrots.

Double Trouble

(HELEN) When Dymond Lake Lodge was still in its fledgling stage it came to pass that there was a weekend with no hunters in camp. Hence, my sister, Louise, flew in with our combined children for a weekend of relaxation. All the guides were about to climb on the plane to leave when Shady, one of the guides, looked around and said, "Just a minute here, if we all leave there will only be you women and children, and there have been a lot of bears around this year." He insisted on staying.

That evening not long after dark, Shady stepped out on the front porch to get a coke from nature's refrigerator, then stopped, and backed carefully into the cabin. We knew immediately what that meant – we had a big white furry visitor! We got out the thunder flashes – and Shady stepped out and threw one behind the bear while Louise and I went into the bedroom where the kids were, to hopefully watch the bear run down the ridge. We threw ourselves up on the top bunk to look out the window and there, just below the window – which is where our underground refrigeration was – was a big white furry rump. I immediately called to Shady and said, "The bear is over here now." His reply was, "If you have a bear over there then we have TWO of them because I can still see this one running down the ridge." By this time we had five little round faces sitting up in their beds with five pairs of "big" eyes. Shady snuck to the corner of the building, threw another thunder flash and the second bear fled with the first. The next morning we found that the dynamic duo had eaten our bacon and butter but had been scared off before they got to Sunday night's turkey!

Vegging Out

Broccoli and Onion Au Gratin

A nice variation on the traditional Broccoli in Cheese Sauce, this is a make-ahead dish that you can make up, refrigerate and pop in the oven in time for dinner. Just remember to add about 10 minutes to the cooking time if it has been refrigerated.

2	onions, thinly sliced	2
1 tbsp.	vegetable oil	15 mL
4 cups	broccoli, blanched*, cut in bite-sized pieces	1 L
2 tbsp.	butter OR margarine	30 mL
2 tbsp.	flour	30 mL
¼ tsp.	salt	1 mL
	dash of pepper	
1 cup	milk	250 mL
4 oz.	cream cheese, cubed	125 mL
2 tbsp.	butter OR margarine	30 mL
⅓ cup	soft bread crumbs	75 mL
2 tbsp.	grated Parmesan cheese	30 mL

1. In a heavy skillet, sauté the onions in the oil until softened.
2. Put the blanched, drained broccoli and onions in a greased 1½-quart (1.5 L) casserole.
3. In a saucepan, melt 2 tbsp. (30 mL) of butter, blend in the flour, salt and pepper. Add the milk and cook and stir until thick and bubbly.
4. Reduce the heat and add the cream cheese, stirring and blending until smooth. Pour over the vegetables.
5. Bake, uncovered, at 350°F (180°C) for 20 minutes.
6. Melt the remaining butter and toss with the bread crumbs and Parmesan cheese. Sprinkle over the casserole and continue baking for another 15 minutes.

Serves 6-8.

* *To blanch vegetables, bring a saucepan of water to a boil, add the vegetables, bring the water back to a full boil and drain immediately. If vegetables are to be further cooked immediately, it is not necessary to plunge them into cold water to stop the cooking process. The cold water preserves color and texture.*

VARIATIONS: You can substitute cauliflower, green beans or asparagus for the broccoli and/or substitute mushrooms for the onions.

Not even a fish would get into trouble if he'd keep his mouth shut!

Creamy Tomato and Onion Surprise

A delicious vegetable recipe that you just throw together, pop in the oven and forget about until dinner is ready.

2 cups	seasoned bread crumbs	500 mL
5	tomatoes, sliced	5
1	medium white onion, sliced	1
½ cup	butter OR margarine	125 mL
3 tbsp.	snipped chives	45 mL
1-2 cups	sour cream	250-500 mL

1. Sprinkle 1 cup (250 mL) of bread crumbs in the bottom of a 9" (23 cm) square casserole. Alternate tomato and onion slices. Dot with half of the butter.
2. Mix the chives with the sour cream. Spread over the tomatoes and onions. Sprinkle with remaining bread crumbs. Dot with the remaining butter.
3. Bake, uncovered, at 350°F (180°C) for 45 minutes.

Serves 6-8.

NOTE: *You can make your own bread crumbs with any flavor of croûtons. Jeanne's Croûtons on page 72 of "Blueberries & Polar Bears" are great!*

Cauliflower Tomato Scallop

An unusual but very good flavor combination! Try the variations also.

⅓ cup	butter OR margarine	75 mL
½ cup	finely chopped celery	125 mL
¼ cup	finely chopped onion	60 mL
¼ cup	finely chopped green pepper	60 mL
¾ tsp.	salt	3 mL
¼ tsp.	pepper	1 mL
¼ cup	flour	60 mL
2 cups	milk	500 mL
1½ cups	shredded sharp Cheddar cheese	375 mL
5 cups	cauliflower florets, blanched*	1.25 L
3	large, firm tomatoes, sliced	3
½ cup	dried bread crumbs	125 mL

Cauliflower Tomato Scallop

Continued

1. Melt the butter in a saucepan and add celery, onion and green pepper. Cook until onion is translucent. Blend in salt, pepper and flour. Gradually add milk, stirring continuously, and cook over low heat until mixture is thickened. Add the cheese and stir until melted. Remove from heat.
2. Arrange half the cauliflower in a shallow 9 x 13" (23 x 33 cm) casserole. Top with a small amount of cheese sauce. Cover with sliced tomatoes and more sauce. Top with remaining cauliflower and sauce. Sprinkle with bread crumbs.
3. Bake, uncovered, at 400°F (200°C) for 25 minutes, or until brown.

Serves 12.

VARIATIONS: BROCCOLI OR ZUCCHINI SCALLOP: You can substitute OR use a combination of broccoli and zucchini with the cauliflower.

* See note on page 139.

Pepper Side Dish

Gavin brought this yummy dish to dinner one night. It's a delightful combination of red, yellow and green peppers, with a little sherry thrown in.

2 tbsp.	olive OR regular vegetable oil	30 mL
½ cup	chunked onion	125 mL
½ cup	chunked celery	125 mL
1	large green pepper, sliced lengthwise	1
1	large red pepper, sliced lengthwise	1
1	large yellow pepper, sliced lengthwise	1
1 cup	sliced mushrooms	250 mL
2 tsp.	DLS*	10 mL
2 tbsp.	dry sherry, optional	30 mL

1. Heat the oil in a large skillet over medium heat.
2. Add the onions and celery and sauté for 3 minutes. Add the peppers and mushrooms and sauté until the vegetables are tender-crisp. Sprinkle with the seasonings while sautéing.
3. Add the sherry, if using, simmer for another minute and serve.

Serves 4.

* Dymond Lake Seasoning. Substitute: ½ tsp. (5 mL) salt, ¼ tsp. (1 mL) EACH of pepper, paprika, thyme, oregano, basil and marjoram.

See photograph on page 17.

Pesto Zucchini

If it is possible, make this pesto sauce with fresh basil – but it is still good with dried basil. Zucchini spread with pesto and cooked tender-crisp – what a taste treat!

Pesto Sauce*:

2 cups	fresh basil OR ½ cup (125 mL) dried	500 mL
2 tsp.	crushed garlic	10 mL
1 tsp.	salt	5 mL
¼ cup	ground pine nuts OR walnuts	60 mL
1 cup	olive oil	250 mL
½ cup	Parmesan cheese	125 mL
2 tbsp.	Romano cheese (optional)	30 mL

zucchini – tender enough to eat with skin on.
Prepare the amount you need.
salt

1. Chop the basil, if using fresh. Mix all the sauce ingredients together.
2. Cut small zucchini in half lengthwise, then cut into 3-4" (7-10 cm) serving pieces. If zucchini is larger, cut it in 1" (2.5 cm) rounds. Place pieces in a lightly greased or sprayed baking dish.
3. Sprinkle zucchini with a little salt. Spread pesto sauce liberally on flat surface of zucchini. There will likely be more sauce then is needed for the zucchini. Cover baking dish and bake at 350°F (180°C) for 20 minutes. Zucchini will be tender-crisp. Do not overbake.

Makes about 2 cups (500 mL) of pesto sauce

* *Refrigerate the remaining sauce in a covered container. It is delicious as a sauce over pasta.*

See photograph on page 155.

Inasmuch as three-quarters of the earth's surface is water and only one-quarter is land, the good Lord's intentions are very clear; a man's time should be divided three quarters for fishing and one quarter for working!

Vegging Out

Ratatouille

What vegetable section would be complete without this favorite vegetable dish from Provence? This recipe comes from an Italian friend and has an authentic European flavor. The only trouble is that she didn't give me any amounts – you'll have to trust my judgement on this one! Oh, yes – be prepared to serve it in individual bowls to hold the flavorful juices!

1	onion,	1
2	green peppers	2
1	eggplant OR 2 zucchini	1
2 cups	fresh mushrooms	500 mL
¼ cup	olive oil	60 mL
2	garlic cloves, crushed	2
28 oz.	can diced tomatoes	796 mL
2 tbsp.	tomato paste	30 mL
¾ tsp.	salt	3 mL
1 tsp.	dried oregano OR 1 tbsp. (15 mL) chopped fresh	5 mL
1 tsp.	dried basil OR 1 tbsp. (15 mL) chopped fresh	5 mL

1. Cut the onion, peppers, eggplant or zucchini and mushrooms into large, bite-sized chunks.
2. Sauté the onions in olive oil for 5 minutes. Add peppers, eggplant or zucchini, mushrooms and garlic and fry for 5 more minutes. Add everything else and simmer for 15-20 minutes.

Serves 6-8.

SERVING SUGGESTION: Ratatouille can be served hot, at room temperature, or chilled. It makes a very good appetizer piled on crusty breads or crackers.

The Fisherman's Prayer

Lord, suffer me to catch a fish
So large that even I,
When talking of it afterwards,
Will have no need to lie!

Very Vegetarian Lasagne

(MARIE) You won't miss the meat in this very flavorful version of lasagne. Helen's in-laws, Garry and Merelyn, make their own noodles as well (wonderful!) – but we use the oven-ready variety – why complicate things?

9-12	lasagne noodles (to cover pan with 3 layers)	9-12
10 oz.	pkg. frozen, chopped spinach, thawed, drained	283 g
2	large carrots, thinly sliced in rings	2
2	large celery stalks, chopped	2
¼ cup	chopped onion	60 mL
2 cups	sliced fresh mushrooms	500 mL
¼ cup	vegetable OR olive oil	60 mL
2	garlic cloves, minced	2
14 oz.	can tomato sauce	398 mL
28 oz.	can tomatoes (plum-type)	796 mL
2 tsp.	white sugar	10 mL
2 tsp.	salt	10 mL
½ tsp.	pepper	2 mL
2	whole cloves	2
1	bay leaf	1
2 tsp.	dried oregano OR 2 tbsp. (30 mL) chopped fresh	10 mL
2 cups	cottage cheese	500 mL
1 cup	Parmesan cheese (freshly grated is best)	250 mL
2 cups	mozzarella cheese, grated	250 mL

1. If you are not using oven-ready, cook the noodles, rinse with cold water, drain and set aside. Prepare the spinach, carrots, celery, onion and mushrooms as indicated above.
2. Gently heat the oil in a large skillet, add the garlic and sauté until brown. Add the carrots, celery and onions; cook just until the onions are translucent, celery and carrots will be slightly crisp.
3. Add tomato sauce, tomatoes, mushrooms, sugar and spices. Cover and simmer for 20 minutes. Discard the bay leaf and cloves.
4. Grease a 9 x 13" (23 x 33 cm) pan and line it with lasagne noodles.
5. Add layers in the following order, using ⅓ tomato sauce, ½ Parmesan cheese, ½ spinach, ½ cottage cheese, noodles. Repeat. Top with last ⅓ of tomato sauce and the mozzarella cheese.
6. Bake 1 hour at 325°F (160°C). Let set for 15 minutes before serving.

Serves 8.

NOTE: This is a good make-ahead dinner. There is a lot of liquid that soaks in by the second day. Before that, sop it up with bread or buns – delicious!

  *Vegging Out*

Tame Meats To Make You Wild

The collection of entrées in this section have withstood the test of time. Many are family favorites, not only because they are delicious, but also because they are easy to prepare with ingredients we already have in our kitchens. Though they range from the "stick-to-your-ribs" variety to the "very elegant", all have also found their way into our menus at the Lodges. Some of our most prestigious company, such as the President of Akjuit Aerospace, the company that is building Spaceport Canada in Churchill, appreciates a good homemade meatloaf as much as the most gourmet fare, as long as we serve it with homemade rolls and Cranberry cake with Butter Sauce – her personal favorite! See "Blueberries & Polar Bears", page 168.

Macho Barbecued Sirloin Steak

(HELEN) Gavin whips up this delicacy for company dinners and we are always happy to partake. He has two methods for cooking it so just use whichever you prefer.

Tangy Soy Marinade:

1 cup	thick barbecue sauce with garlic	500 mL
2 tbsp.	soy sauce	30 mL
2 tsp.	mustard, regular OR Dijon	10 mL
2 tsp.	horseradish	10 mL
2 tsp.	lemon juice	10 mL
2 tsp.	jalapeño juice (from jalapeño pickles)	10 mL
1 tbsp.	finely chopped onion	15 mL
2 tsp.	DLS* or 1 tsp. (5 mL) seasoned pepper	10 mL
1	2-2¼" (5-5.5 cm) sirloin steak (no thinner)	1

1. Make a marinade with the barbecue sauce, soy sauce, mustard, horse-radish, lemon juice, jalapeño juice, onion and DLS*.
2. Place the steak in a glass or plastic container and pour the marinade over. Let sit in the refrigerator or in a cool place at least 6 hours, overnight if you like. Turn occasionally.
3. Heat the barbecue to high. Remove the steak from the marinade; place on the hot barbecue and close the lid. Sear well on both sides brushing frequently with the marinade. When steak is well seared, approximately 10 minutes, you can do one of 2 things. You can place the steak in a shallow roaster and put it in the oven at 325°F (160°C) to finish cooking. Be sure to brush with the leftover marinade every 15 minutes. It will take 30-45 minutes to finish cooking. If you prefer to finish it on the barbecue, turn the barbecue down to medium and continue to turn and baste until it reaches the desired doneness.
4. To serve, cut steak into serving pieces.

Serves 6.

HINT: Buy a sirloin tip or top sirloin roast and cut your own steaks. There is lots of sauce to do more than 1 steak.

* *Dymond Lake Seasoning*

Steak and Kidney Pie

(HELEN) My brother-in-law, John, came to us from Scotland, via northern Ontario. He was a "Bay" boy who landed in Churchill and forgot to leave for quite awhile. Anyway, this is one of his favorites and I know I won't go wrong if I make this when he is coming for dinner.

2 lbs.	round steak, cut in cubes	1 kg
⅓ cup	flour	75 mL
¼ cup	vegetable oil	60 mL
½ lb.	beef kidney, cut in very small pieces	250 g
½ cup	chopped onion	125 mL
1	garlic clove, minced	1
2 cups	beef stock	500 mL
1 cup	dry red wine	250 mL
2 tbsp.	tomato paste	30 mL
1 tbsp.	DLS* or 2 tsp. (10 mL) salt and ½ tsp. (2 mL) pepper	15 mL
½ tsp.	dried rosemary OR 1 tbsp. (15 mL) chopped fresh	2 mL
½ tsp.	dried oregano OR 1 tbsp. (15 mL) chopped fresh	2 mL
	pie pastry for a single-crust pie	

1. Dredge steak with flour. Heat the oil in a large, heavy frying pan over medium-high heat. Add the steak and cook until well browned all over. Add the kidney and brown.
2. Stir in the onions and garlic and cook until onions are just tender.
3. Add the stock, wine, tomato paste, and seasonings.
4. Cook, uncovered, until sauce is smooth and thickened. Be sure to stir often. When sauce is slightly thickened, reduce the heat and cover the pan. Simmer for 1 hour, or until meat is tender. Stir occasionally.
5. If the stew is too thick, thin with more stock or wine. Place stew in a greased 10" (25 cm) pie plate or 2-quart (2 L) casserole and chill. If you do this a day ahead, cover the stew and refrigerate until you are ready to add the crust and bake.
6. To bake, roll out the pastry and fit over the baking dish. Seal edges, Brush with egg and cut steam vents in the top.
7. Bake at 400°F (200°C) for 35 minutes, or until pastry is golden brown and filling is bubbly in the middle.

Serves 8.

* *Dymond Lake Seasoning*

Braised Short Ribs

This is by far the best recipe that I have ever found for short ribs. They are tender, juicy and oh so good. I have also used this recipe with lamb ribs with very good results.

6 lbs.	beef short ribs	2.5 kg
2 tbsp.	cooking oil	30 mL
1	large onion, chopped	1
⅓ cup	dry red wine	75 mL
2 tsp.	horseradish	10 mL
1 tsp.	paprika	5 mL
1 tsp.	DLS* or ¼ tsp. (1 mL) pepper	1 mL
2 tbsp.	fresh lemon juice	30 mL
2 cups	beef stock	500 mL
¼ cup	flour	60 mL
½ cup	water	125 mL
1 tsp.	sugar	5 mL
2 tsp.	dillweed	10 mL

1. Trim the excess fat from the meat and cut the ribs into serving-sized pieces.
2. Heat the oil in a Dutch oven over medium heat. Brown the meat on all sides. Remove the meat from the pan and pour off all but 2 tbsp. (30 mL) of the fat.
3. Add the onions to the pan and cook until they are limp. Add the wine, horseradish, paprika, DLS*, lemon juice and stock. Return the meat to the pan.
4. Cover and bake at 325°F (160°C) for 2½-3 hours, or until tender.
5. Remove the meat from the pan. Trim away any visible fat and remove the bones which should be falling out at this point. Remove all the fat from the liquid in the pan. Measure the pan liquid and add water to make 2½ cups (625 mL). Pour the liquid back into the pan.
6. Add the ¼ cup (60 mL) of flour to an additional ½ cup (125 mL) of cold water. Mix until smooth. Add to the pan mixture along with the sugar and dillweed. Bring to a boil, stirring constantly.
7. Return the meat to the pan, cover and return to the oven for another 30 minutes.

Serves 4-6.

SERVING SUGGESTION: *This is great served with our Creamy Oven-Mashed Potatoes, page 131, "Blueberries & Polar Bears".*

* *Dymond Lake Seasoning*

Tame Meats

Enchiladas

(HELEN) I spent two years of high school in Arizona where Mexican food abounds and never tried an enchilada. Years later, I found this recipe, and we love them.

Thin Pancakes: (small flour tortillas may be substituted)

6	eggs, well beaten	6
3 cups	milk	750 mL
2 cups	flour	500 mL
¾ tsp.	salt	3 mL

Chili Beef Filling and Sauce:

2 lbs.	ground beef (or combinations of beef, pork, moose, caribou, deer OR whatever you have on hand)	1 kg
1 cup	chopped onion	250 mL
½ cup	chopped green pepper	125 mL
2	garlic cloves, minced	2
2 tbsp.	chili powder	30 mL
1 tsp.	salt	5 mL
10 oz.	pkg. frozen spinach, cooked, drained and chopped	283 g
28 oz.	jar meatless spaghetti sauce	796 mL
1 cup	tomato sauce	250 mL
1 cup	water	250 mL
1 tbsp.	chili powder	15 mL
2 cups	shredded Cheddar cheese	500 mL

1. To make the pancakes, combine the eggs and milk in a bowl. Add the flour and salt and beat until smooth.
2. Pour about ¼ cup (60 mL) batter into a hot, greased, 6-7" (15-18 cm) skillet, tilting skillet so the batter covers the surface. The batter can also be spread into 6" (15 cm) rounds on a greased skillet. Turn the pancakes when the surface looks dry.
3. Cooked pancakes can be stacked with waxed paper between each to keep them from sticking. Set pancakes aside and prepare the filling.
4. To prepare filling, brown meat in a large frying pan. Pour off all but 1 tbsp. (15 mL) of fat. Add onion, green pepper, garlic, chili powder and salt. Simmer for 10 minutes. Mix in spinach. Let cool.
5. To make the sauce, combine the spaghetti sauce, tomato sauce, water and 1 tbsp. (15 mL) of chili powder. Set aside.
6. Spoon ¼ cup (60 mL) of meat mixture across the center of each pancake. Fold sides over about ½" (1.3 cm) and roll up each pancake.
7. Place filled pancakes in 2 greased, 9 x 13" (23 x 33 cm) baking pans. Pour half the sauce over each; top each with half of the cheese.
8. Bake in a 325°F (160°C) oven for 30 minutes, or until hot and bubbly.

Makes 30 enchiladas. Serves 8-10.

SERVING SUGGESTION: The prepared enchiladas can be frozen. To reheat, bake at 375°F (190°C) for 45 minutes, or until hot and bubbly.

Tame Meats

149

Mexican Lasagne

Indescribably delicious, this lasagne is built on tortillas. Make it as hot or mild as you like by using mild, medium or hot salsa and taco sauce. Team it up with this super guacamole and watch it disappear!

1 lb.	lean ground beef	500 g
¼ cup	taco seasoning	60 mL
10	10" (25 cm) flour tortillas	10
14 oz.	can refried beans	398 mL
2 cups	grated Monterey Jack cheese OR mozzarella	500 mL
1 cup	salsa	250 mL
½ cup	chopped OR sliced green pepper	125 mL
¾ cup	taco sauce	175 mL

1. In a frying pan, sauté beef until browned, pour off fat and stir in taco seasoning.
2. Spray 10" (25 cm) springform pan with nonstick spray or grease lightly.
3. Place 2 tortillas in the pan and cover with half of the meat mixture.
4. Cover meat with 2 more tortillas and spread over the refried beans and 1 cup (250 mL) of the cheese.
5. Place 2 more tortillas in the pan and cover with the salsa and peppers.
6. Place 2 more tortillas in the pan; cover with remaining meat mixture.
7. Place the last 2 tortillas in the pan. Cover with the taco sauce and the remaining 1 cup (250 mL) of cheese.
8. Cover with foil and bake at 350°F (180°C) for 45 minutes.
9. Remove from oven; run a knife around the edge before removing pan collar. Cut into wedges and serve with the guacamole (below).

Serves 6-8.

NOTE: Can be made a day ahead and refrigerated.

Guacamole ¡Estupendo!

2	ripe avocados	2
1 tbsp.	lime juice	15 mL
2	garlic cloves, crushed	2
1 tbsp.	finely chopped pickled jalapeño pepper	15 mL
1 cup	sour cream	250 mL
⅛ tsp.	ground cumin	0.5 mL
¼ tsp.	salt	1 mL
1	large tomato, chopped and left in a sieve to drain for a couple of minutes	1
3	green onions, chopped	3
1	large green pepper, chopped	1

Tame Meats

1. Peel and mash the avocados. Add the lime juice immediately and then add the garlic, jalapeño, sour cream, cumin and salt. Mix well with an electric mixer. Add tomatoes, onion and green pepper and mix by hand. Chill for 2 hours.

Makes about 3 cups (750 mL).

Marie's Meat Loaf

(MARIE) This is the first recipe I ever collected – from the mother of an old boyfriend. (Some things endure the test of time better than young love!) The poultry seasoning adds a distinctive flavor. The leftovers are great sliced thinly for sandwiches.

2 lbs.	ground beef	1 kg
¼ cup	finely chopped onion	60 mL
2 tbsp.	finely chopped celery	30 mL
2 tsp.	DLS*	10 mL
1 tsp.	salt	5 mL
½ tsp.	poultry seasoning	2 mL
¼ tsp.	dry mustard	1 mL
1 tbsp.	Worcestershire sauce	15 mL
4	slices soft bread, cubed	4
½ cup	milk	125 mL
2	eggs, beaten	2
½ cup	dry bread crumbs	125 mL
¼ cup	chili sauce OR ketchup	60 mL
½ cup	boiling water	125 mL

1. Mix beef with the onion, celery, seasonings and Worcestershire sauce.
2. Add the bread cubes to milk, let soak a minute or 2 and add the beaten eggs. Mix well with the beef mixture.
3. Shape into a loaf, roll in the dry bread crumbs and place in a greased 5 x 9" (13 x 23 cm) loaf pan. Make diagonal slits in the top and fill them with chili sauce or ketchup.
4. Pour the boiling water around the loaf and bake, uncovered, at 350°F (180°C) for 1 hour.

Serves 6.

* *Dymond Lake Seasoning – If you don't have DLS, increase the salt to 2 tsp. (10 mL) and add ¼ tsp. (1 mL) of pepper.*

Beef Tostadas

Toni came up with this recipe for one of our Mexican nights at North Knife Lake. It was rated a keeper (fishermen's lingo) and has now become a regular.

Chili Beef Filling:

4 lb.	beef pot roast	2 kg
	DLS* or seasoned salt and pepper	
1	garlic clove, crushed	1
1 tbsp.	chili powder	15 mL
4 cups	tomato sauce	1 L
1 tbsp.	taco seasoning	15 mL
1 tsp.	Cajun seasoning	5 mL
1	garlic clove, crushed	1
1 tsp.	chili powder	5 mL
1 tsp.	Italian seasoning	5 mL
1 tbsp.	Worcestershire sauce	15 mL
1 cup	chopped onion	250 mL
1 cup	chopped green pepper	250 mL
1 cup	chopped red pepper	250 mL

crisp corn tortilla shells (3-4 per person)
sour cream for garnish
diced tomatoes for garnish
diced green pepper for garnish
diced onions for garnish

1. Place the roast on a sheet of heavy foil. Sprinkle liberally with DLS*, crushed garlic and 1 tbsp. (15 mL) chili powder. Wrap the foil tightly around the roast and seal. Place on a baking sheet and roast at 250°F (120°C) for 5 hours, or until meat falls apart. You could also do this step in a slow cooker.
2. Combine the rest of the filling ingredients in a heavy saucepan. Simmer over low heat for 30 minutes.
3. When the roast is done, shred it and add to the sauce. Simmer for 15-20 minutes.
4. Warm the tortilla shells in the oven for a couple of minutes and then let your guests (or family) put their own tostadas together and garnish them as they like. To make tostadas, spoon beef filling into shells and add your favorite toppings.

Serves 10-12.

NOTE: Excess filling may be frozen.

* *Dymond Lake Seasoning*

  Tame Meats

Cheddar Cheese Tourtière

(HELEN) We have started a new tradition in the last couple of years. I still have two sisters and a brother living in Churchill. We show up at my mom's house on Christmas Eve for a very casual potluck supper. I always bring a couple of cheesy meat pies which I've made and frozen earlier in December. They are good any time of the year, though, and our hunters and fishermen especially enjoy them.

The recipe calls for ground beef but don't be afraid to substitute pork, moose, caribou or deer if you have it on hand.

2 lbs.	ground beef	1 kg
2 tbsp.	vegetable oil	30 mL
1 cup	chopped onion	250 mL
½ cup	chopped celery	125 mL
2 tsp.	DLS*	10 mL
2 tsp.	sage	10 mL
¼ tsp.	ground cloves	1 mL
½ tsp.	minced garlic	2 mL
1½ cups	mashed potatoes (approximately)	375 mL
	pie pastry for 2 double-crust pies**	
2 tbsp.	fine, dry breadcrumbs	30 mL
3 cups	grated Cheddar cheese	750 mL

1. In a frying pan, brown the meat in the oil. Remove the meat to a large bowl and sauté the onions and celery. Drain well and add to the meat mixture.
2. To the meat mixture add the DLS*, sage, ground cloves, garlic and mashed potatoes. Mix well.
3. Line 2, 9" (23 cm) pie plates with pastry. Sprinkle each with 1 tbsp. (15 mL) of the bread crumbs. Put ¼ of the meat filling in the bottom of each pie crust. Divide the cheese between the 2 pies and then cover with the remainder of the meat filling. Cover with the top crust and seal the edges. Cut 3 slits in the top of each crust to let the steam escape.
4. Bake the pies at 425°F (220°C) for 30 minutes, or until the crust is golden brown. If you have frozen the pies unbaked, be sure to defrost them before baking and add about 20 minutes to the cooking time.

Cut each pie into 6 pieces. Two pies serve 8-10 people.

SERVING SUGGESTIONS: This is great served with Chili Sauce, page 200, and Simply Delicious Apple Coleslaw, page 125.

* *Dymond Lake Seasoning. You can substitute 1 tsp. (5 mL) EACH of seasoned salt and seasoned pepper.*
** *See "Blueberries & Polar Bears", page 184.*

Cornish Pasties

(Marie) This is another family favorite. Besides their great flavor we like them for their convenience. Easy because you don't precook the filling and convenient to have in the freezer for unexpected company.

2 lbs.	lean ground beef	1 kg
4 cups	diced unpeeled potatoes	1 L
3 cups	chopped onion	750 mL
½ cup	minced parsley	125 mL
2 tsp.	salt	10 mL
2 tsp.	paprika	10 mL
2 tsp.	soy sauce	10 mL
	pastry for 3, 2-crust pies*	
1	egg	1
1 tbsp.	water	15 mL

1. In a large bowl mix the beef, potatoes, onion, parsley, salt, paprika and soy sauce.
2. Divide the pastry into 3 parts. Roll out 1 ball and cut into rounds using a 5-6" (13-15 cm) bowl or can**.
3. Whisk the egg and water together with a fork.
4. Brush the edges of each pastry round with the egg mixture. Spoon ½ cup (125 mL) of filling onto the pastry. Fold pastry in half and press edges together. Crimp with a fork. Cut 3 slits in each to let steam escape.
5. Bake 10 minutes at 400°F (200°C). Turn the oven down to 325°F (160°C) and continue to cook for 30 minutes.

Makes 2 dozen.

NOTE: You can freeze these either cooked or uncooked. If you freeze them uncooked just increase the 30 minutes at 325°F (160°C) by 5-10 minutes.

* *See "Blueberries & Polar Bears", page 184.*
** *Pasty makers are now available to make this job much easier.*

Wild Game – Goose

Goose à l'Orange, page 24
  with Cranberry Orange Relish, page 199
Garlicky Mashed Potatoes, page 133
Pesto Zucchini, page 142
Cream Cheese with Golden Caviar, page 28

Saucy Lemon Pork Chops

This recipe was scribbled on a piece of paper that was covered with blotches and grease spots – the type of recipe you know has been used over and over again.

6	pork chops, ¾" (2 cm) thick	6
2 tbsp.	oil	30 mL
	DLS* or salt and seasoned pepper	
½	lemon, thinly sliced	½
6	large slices of onion	6
1 cup	water	250 mL
⅓ cup	brown sugar	75 mL
⅓ cup	white vinegar	75 mL
½ cup	ketchup	125 mL

1. Season pork chops with DLS* then fry them, in hot oil, until nicely browned on both sides. Trim and discard excess fat. Place the pork chops in a 2-3-quart (2-3 L) casserole or baking pan.
2. Place the lemon and onion slices over the pork chops. (They can be layered.)
3. Pour 1 cup (250 mL) of water into the frying pan to blend with the meat juices.
4. Add the sugar, vinegar and ketchup to the pan juices. Pour over the pork chops and cover.
5. Bake in a 350°F (180°C) oven for 1 hour, or until the chops are tender.

Serves 4-6.

NOTE: These are even better reheated, so don't be afraid to double the recipe for leftovers.

SERVING SUGGESTION: Serve these with French Fries or Crispy Round Oven Fries, page 131, and kernel corn. The sauce complements these vegetables.

* Dymond Lake Seasoning

Canada geese over Dymond Lake at twilight.

Sweet and Pungent Pork

This recipe was handed down from Marie's mother. It is quick, easy and delicious. Kids like it too!

1 lb.	pork tenderloin, cut in ½" (1.3 cm) cubes	500 g
2 tbsp.	flour	30 mL
2 tbsp.	vegetable oil	30 mL
¼ cup	chopped onion	60 mL
1 tsp.	salt	5 mL
⅛ tsp.	pepper	0.5 mL
14 oz.	can pineapple, crushed OR tidbits	398 mL
1¼ cups	beef stock	300 mL
3 tbsp.	cornstarch	45 mL
¼ cup	cider vinegar	60 mL
1 tsp.	soy sauce	5 mL
¼ cup	brown sugar	60 mL
2	green peppers, cut in strips	2
3 cups	hot cooked rice	750 mL

1. Heat the oil in a heavy skillet over medium heat. Dredge the pork in flour and brown in oil.
2. Add the onions, salt, pepper, pineapple with juice and half the beef stock. Cover and simmer for 30 minutes.
3. Blend the cornstarch with the remaining stock and add to the pork with the vinegar, soy sauce and brown sugar. Stir until smooth. Add the green peppers; stir, cover and simmer for 15 minutes.
4. Heap the rice in a ring on the serving platter and pour the pork into the center.

Serves 4.

Herbed Lemon Pork Chops

One of those couldn't-be-easier recipes that is fit for your finest company. When we serve them at the lodge we have to make sure we have plenty!.

minced garlic
pork chops, cut 1" (2.5 cm) thick
DLS*
oregano
basil
lemon juice

Herbed Lemon Pork Chops

Continued

1. Rub garlic over the chops, on both sides and sprinkle liberally on both sides with the DLS*, oregano and basil.
2. Place chops on a greased baking sheet and squeeze or pour lemon juice over them. Be generous.
3. Bake at 350°F (180°C) for 45-60 minutes. Don't overcook chops or they will be dry.

SERVING SUGGESTION: Team up with Paprika Potatoes, page 132, and Waldorf Salad, page 125.

*   For Dymond Lake Seasoning substitute salt and seasoned pepper.

Honey Garlic Ribs

(HELEN) Where would we be without our families? This recipe comes from Marie's sister-in-law, Diane, whose family runs a restaurant in Brantford, Ontario. You will notice that there is no honey in these ribs but you wouldn't know it to taste them. Enjoy – this is finger food!

3 lbs.	pork ribs, cut for sweet 'n' sour	1.5 kg
½ tsp.	oil	2 mL
¼ cup	soy sauce	60 mL
1 tbsp.	water	15 mL
¼ cup	sugar	60 mL
1	garlic clove, crushed	1

1. Cut ribs into bite-sized pieces (between each bone). Place the ribs in a shallow baking pan and brown in the oven at 400°F (200°C), turning once after 15 minutes. This will take about 30 minutes.
2. Put ½ tsp. (2 mL) of oil into a saucepan and add the soy sauce, water, sugar and garlic. Bring it to a boil, then turn down heat and simmer until the sauce is almost thick, about 5 minutes. Remove from the heat.
3. When the ribs are browned, remove them from the oven and pour off any juice in the bottom. Brush the sauce over the ribs, using a pastry brush, to be sure they are all covered.
4. Lower the oven temperature to 375°F (190°C) and continue to cook the ribs for 30-45 minutes. Stir them every 15 minutes.

Serves 4.

Veal Parmesan

(HELEN) When I asked Toni to fax me this recipe, it came with a note on it that read, "from the only daughter who didn't make it into the first cookbook." An oversight that we are definitely correcting this time around. This is a recipe which Toni developed that has become a favorite at North Knife and at home too.

3 x 14 oz.	cans tomato sauce	3 x 398 mL
2 tsp.	dried basil OR 2 tbsp. (30 mL) chopped fresh	10 mL
1 tsp.	Italian seasoning	5 mL
¼ tsp.	dried oregano OR ¾ tsp. (3 mL) chopped fresh	1 mL
1 tbsp.	Worcestershire sauce	15 mL
1	garlic clove, minced	1
1 tsp.	beef bouillon powder OR 1 cube	5 mL
⅓ cup	chopped onion	75 mL
⅓ cup	chopped celery	75 mL
⅓ cup	chopped green pepper	75 mL
⅓ cup	chopped red pepper	75 mL
½ cup	flour	125 mL
½ cup	cornflake crumbs	125 mL
½ cup	Parmesan cheese	125 mL
1 tsp.	DLS* OR ½ tsp. (3 mL) salt and ¼ tsp. (1 mL) pepper	5 mL
6	6 oz. (170 g) veal cutlets	6
3	eggs, beaten	3
	olive oil OR butter	
¼ cup	Parmesan cheese	60 mL
½ cup	grated mozzarella	125 mL

1. In heavy saucepan, combine the tomato sauce, basil, Italian seasoning, oregano, Worcestershire sauce, garlic, beef bouillon and vegetables. Simmer for 30-45 minutes, stirring occasionally.
2. Meanwhile, mix the flour, cornflake crumbs, ½ cup (125 mL) Parmesan cheese and seasoning. Dip the cutlets in the beaten eggs and then the crumb mixture. Be sure to completely coat the cutlets.
3. Heat ¼ cup (60 mL) of olive oil or butter in a heavy skillet over medium-high heat. Quickly brown the cutlets on both sides and then remove to a 9 x 13" (23 x 33 cm) ovenproof dish.
4. Pour tomato sauce over cutlets; bake at 350°F (180°C) for 45 minutes.
5. Sprinkle with ¼ cup (60 mL) of Parmesan and the mozzarella cheese before serving.

Serves 6.

SERVING SUGGESTION: This makes a very impressive meal served with a Greek Salad and pasta dish! For a thriftier meal, use pork or turkey cutlets.

* Dymond Lake Seasoning

  Tame Meats

Feta-Stuffed Chicken Breasts

Feta cheese and pine nuts, how many of us had even heard of them in Canada 20 years ago? Now they show up everywhere and we are glad they do. They are a great combination in this dish.

2 tsp.	olive oil	10 mL
¼ cup	chopped onion	60 mL
1	garlic clove, crushed	1
10 oz.	pkg. frozen spinach, chopped, drained (not too dry)	283 g
⅔ cup	crumbled feta cheese	150 ml
1 tbsp.	pine nuts	15 mL
1 tbsp.	snipped fresh dill OR 1 tsp. (5 mL) dried	15 mL
	black pepper	
4	skinless, boneless chicken breasts	4
	water	
¼ cup	flour	60 mL
¼ cup	Parmesan cheese	60 mL
1 tsp.	DLS* OR ½ tsp. (2 mL) salt and ¼ tsp. (1 mL) pepper	5 mL
	vegetable or olive oil	

1. Heat the olive oil in a heavy skillet. Add the onion, garlic, spinach, feta cheese, pine nuts, dill and black pepper. Sauté for 5 minutes and set aside.
2. Pound the chicken breasts to ¼" (6 mm) thickness. Put one-eighth of the filling in the middle of each cutlet. Fold in the ends and roll up, completely enclosing the filling, if possible. Secure with toothpicks.
3. Brush with water and roll in mixture of flour, Parmesan and DLS*.
4. Place on a greased 9 x 13" (23 x 33 cm) pan. Bake for 20 minutes at 375°F (190°C). Brush with oil. Bake 20 minutes more.

Serves 4.

* *Dymond Lake Seasoning*

Goose Facts – Who Says Birds Can't Count?

Wherever you see large numbers of geese gathered, they are formed into smaller groups. These may be families, pairs, singles, or a group of yearlings. A hierarchy exists which gives the highest status to the gander with the most goslings. The more goslings in a family group, the more aggressive is the gander. Fights only occur between ganders of equal rank, i.e. with the same number of goslings!

Tarragon Mushroom Chicken

A hint of tarragon in a thin creamy mushroom sauce – enough to serve over noodles – succulent and simple!

12	chicken pieces	12
	butter, melted	
	DLS* OR salt and seasoned pepper	
3 tbsp.	butter OR margarine	45 mL
4 cups	sliced, fresh mushrooms OR 2 x 10 oz.	1 L
	(2 x 284 mL) cans, with juice	
¼ cup	flour	60 mL
1½ cups	chicken stock	375 mL
½ tsp.	dried tarragon OR 1 tbsp. (15 mL) minced fresh	2 mL
¾ cup	light cream OR evaporated milk	175 mL
¼ cup	white wine (optional)	60 mL
	salt and pepper to taste	

1. Arrange the chicken pieces, skin side up, on a greased baking tray. Brush with melted butter and sprinkle **generously** with DLS, or salt and seasoned pepper.
2. Bake at 375°F (190°C) for 30-40 minutes, or until skin is WELL BROWNED. Remove chicken to a 4-5-quart (4-5 L) casserole.
3. Melt butter and sauté the mushrooms. Sprinkle with the flour and stir, blending well. Gradually add the chicken broth, stirring continually to keep the sauce smooth. Add the tarragon and cook until thickened. Add cream and wine, then season to taste.
4. Pour the sauce over the chicken in the casserole. Bake, uncovered, at 350°F (180°C) for 30 minutes.

Serves 6.

NOTE: Increase baking time to 1 hour if you have made chicken ahead and refrigerated it.

SERVING SUGGESTION: This chicken is great served over noodles with Minted Green Bean Salad, page 120.

* *Dymond Lake Seasoning*

An old man was on the bank of a river, fishing out of season. Sensing a presence behind him, he turned to see a man in uniform. "You the game warden?" he asked. "Yep!" came the reply. The old man nodded to the minnow on the line he had just lifted from the water. "Just teaching him to swim!"

Herb-Roasted Chicken

What can we say about this dish except that it smells wonderful when it is cooking and tastes just as wonderful to eat. Team it up with Tomatoes Vinaigrette, page 118, Baked Potato – What a Slice!, page 132, and Nifty Carrots, page 136.

4 lb.	roasting chicken	2 kg
1	garlic clove, crushed	1
1 tsp.	dried rosemary leaves OR 1 tbsp. (15 mL) fresh	5 mL
1 tsp.	dried thyme leaves OR 1 tbsp. (15 mL) fresh	5 mL
1 tsp.	dried oregano OR marjoram leaves OR 2 tbsp. (30 mL) fresh	5 mL
¼ tsp.	pepper	1 mL
½ tsp.	salt	2 mL
1 tbsp.	olive oil	15 mL

1. Wash chicken and pat dry.
2. Mix garlic with rosemary, thyme, oregano, pepper, salt and oil.
3. Using a pastry brush, brush herb mixture over the entire surface of the chicken.
4. Place the chicken on a rack in a roaster. Roast, breast side up, at 375°F (190°C) for 20 minutes. Turn chicken over, breast side down, baste with drippings and roast another 20 minutes. Turn over once again so that the breast is up, baste with drippings and roast an additional 35 minutes, or until done.
5. Remove the chicken from the oven, set in a warm place and cover with a foil tent. Let rest 15 minutes before carving.

Serves 4.

Goose Facts – Adoption or Birdnapping?

Occasionally 2-year-olds will breed (though 3 years is more common). When that happens, they are likely to lose their brood to an older, more aggressive pair – sometimes their own parents – thus forming a "gang brood" of 10 to 20 goslings. More goslings equals higher status. Talk about a power trip!

Chicken Stir-Fry with Ginger Soy Sauce

(HELEN) From my daughter Toni, a zesty ginger soy sauce to dress up the chicken and vegetables.

Ginger Soy Sauce:

1 tbsp.	cornstarch	15 mL
2 tbsp.	water	30 mL
¼ cup	red wine vinegar	60 mL
¼ cup	soy sauce	60 mL
2 tbsp.	brown sugar	30 mL
1 tbsp.	finely chopped fresh ginger OR ⅛ tsp. (0.5 mL) ground ginger	15 mL
2 tbsp.	vegetable oil	30 mL
2 lbs.	boneless, skinless chicken breasts cut in thin strips	1 kg
	DLS* OR salt & pepper	
1 tbsp.	vegetable oil	15 mL
1 cup	diagonally-cut carrots	250 mL
⅓ cup	diagonally-cut celery	75 mL
⅓ cup	chunked onions	75 mL
1 cup	sliced fresh mushrooms	250 mL
1	garlic clove, minced	1
1 cup	cauliflower florets	250 mL
⅓ cup	green pepper cut in strips	75 mL

1. To make the sauce, mix together the cornstarch and water until smooth. Add the vinegar, soy sauce, brown sugar and ginger.
2. Heat 1 tbsp. (15 mL) of oil in a wok or large skillet to medium high. Add half the chicken, season to taste and stir-fry for approximately 5 minutes, until chicken is just cooked. Remove chicken from pan and set aside. Repeat with 1 tbsp. (15 mL) oil and remaining chicken.
3. Add 1 more tbsp. (15 mL) oil to pan. Add the carrots, celery, onion, mushrooms, garlic and cauliflower. Stir-fry until tender-crisp, approximately 5 minutes. Add green pepper for the last minute only.
4. Add the sauce mixture to the chicken and vegetables and stir constantly until mixture comes to a boil and thickens.

Serves 4-6.

VARIATION: Always versatile, stir-fries can include whatever vegetables you have to hand. Add broccoli, zucchini, red and yellow peppers, green onion, to vary the color and flavors.

  Tame Meats

Elegant Mushroom Chicken

The Duchess of Windsor is credited with saying "you can never be too rich or too thin". Well, I'm not sure about that but I do think you can never have too many "good" chicken recipes. This one is not only elegant but easy!

¼ cup	butter OR margarine	60 mL
1 cup	chopped celery	250 mL
1	garlic clove, crushed	1
6 tbsp.	flour	90 mL
3 cups	milk	750 mL
8 oz.	cream cheese, cubed	250 g
½ cup	chopped pimiento	125 mL
½ cup	sliced stuffed olives	125 mL
½ tsp.	salt	2 mL
1 tsp.	lemon pepper	5 mL
1 tbsp.	chopped, fresh thyme OR ½ tsp. (2 mL) dried	15 mL
2 tbsp.	butter OR margarine	30 mL
4 cups	sliced fresh mushrooms	1 L
12	single chicken breasts, boneless, skinless, cut in cubes	12
1 cup	bread crumbs	250 mL
3 tbsp.	butter OR margarine, melted	45 mL

1. Melt the butter in a skillet over medium heat. Add the celery and garlic. Sauté for 3-4 minutes but do not brown the garlic.
2. Add the flour and mix until smooth. Add the milk and bring to a boil. Add cream cheese and stir until smooth. Remove from the heat and add the pimiento, olives, salt, lemon pepper and thyme.
3. Melt the next 2 tbsp. (30 mL) of butter and sauté the mushrooms for 3 minutes. Add to the creamed mixture with the cubed chicken.
4. Pour the mixture into a greased 9 x 13" (23 x 3 cm) casserole. Top with the bread crumbs tossed with 3 tbsp. (45 mL) of melted butter.
5. Bake at 350°F (180°C) for 60 minutes.

Serves 10-12.

A woman was bemoaning the fact that her husband had left her for the fifth time. "Never mind," consoled the neighbor. "He'll be back again." "Not this time," cried the wife. "He took all his fishing equipment with him!"

White Clam Linguine

(HELEN) Shari passed this one on from her father-in-law, Larry. Her comment was, "I didn't like clams but I love this dish." It is very simple to prepare but very impressive to serve.

¼ cup	butter OR margarine	60 mL
½ cup	chopped onion	125 mL
2	garlic cloves, minced	2
2 tbsp.	flour	30 mL
1 cup	clam juice (from clams)	250 mL
1 cup	half-and-half cream	250 mL
1½ cups	sliced mushrooms	375 mL
1 tbsp.	chopped parsley	15 mL
½ tsp.	dried oregano OR 1 tbsp. (15 mL) chopped fresh	2 mL
½ tsp.	dried thyme OR 1 tbsp. (15 mL) chopped fresh	2 mL
½ tsp.	red pepper flakes	2 mL
1 tsp.	DLS*	5 mL
2 x 5 oz.	cans clams, drained, reserve juice – should be 2 cups (500 mL) of clams	2 x 142 g
	cooked linguine for 4	

1. Melt the butter in a heavy saucepan over medium heat. Add the onions and garlic and cook until the onions are translucent.
2. Remove the pan from the heat and add the flour. Stir until smooth and gradually add the clam juice, using a whisk. Add the half-and-half, mushrooms and seasonings. Return to the heat; cook and stir until mixture comes to a boil. Simmer, stirring constantly, for 2 minutes.
3. Remove from the heat and stir in the clams just before serving.
4. Serve over linguine noodles.

Serves 4.

* *Dymond Lake Seasoning or substitute ½ tsp. (2 mL) seasoned pepper.*

Three men were out in a canoe. It tipped over and dunked them all right under. All but one got his hair wet. Why?

(Because he was bald.)

  *Tame Meats*

Final Temptations

Dessert is something that we never have complaints about at the Lodges – lots of moans – ("Oh, no! Another great dessert. They're irresistible!") but no complaints. There are so many to choose from, that only a few get repeated on a regular basis. And you won't find much here to interest a serious dieter – the only diet up north is to take a smaller piece than what you really want!

White Chocolate Cranberry Cake

Just a hint of chocolate comes through in this cranberry cake, which contrasts the sweetness of white chocolate with the tartness of cranberries. A white chocolate and orange glaze completes the ensemble. Very subtle.

1 cup	butter OR margarine	250 mL
1 cup	brown sugar	250 mL
½ cup	white sugar	125 mL
4	eggs	4
3 tbsp.	orange juice	45 mL
1 tbsp.	grated orange rind	15 mL
2 cups	flour	500 mL
2 tsp.	baking powder	10 mL
1½ cups	cranberries, fresh OR frozen	375 mL
6 x 1 oz.	squares white chocolate, chopped	6 x 30 g
	white chocolate curls	

White Chocolate and Orange Glaze:

3 x 1 oz.	squares white chocolate OR ½ cup (125 mL)	3 x 30 g
	white chocolate chips	
2 tbsp.	orange juice	30 mL

1. In a large bowl, beat butter and sugars with an electric mixer.
2. Add eggs, orange juice and rind and beat well. Add flour and baking powder and beat well.
3. Stir in cranberries and chopped chocolate.
4. Turn batter into a greased and floured 10" (25 cm) tube or bundt pan. Bake at 350°F (180°C) for 60-70 minutes, or until a toothpick inserted in center comes out clean. Cool in the pan for 10 minutes, then turn out onto a cooling rack.
5. To make the glaze, melt the white chocolate and orange juice over low heat or in the microwave on medium for 1½ minutes. Stir until smooth. Drizzle the glaze over the cooled cake. Garnish with white chocolate curls.

Serves 12-16.

NOTE: One package of white chocolate contains 6 squares. Six squares chopped equals 1 cup (250 mL) of chocolate chips.

See photograph on page 173.

  Final Temptations

Grand Marnier Bundt Cake

This delightful cake is simple yet superb – with tingle-your-tastebuds appeal.

Grand Marnier Syrup:

¼ cup	slivered fresh orange peel	60 mL
1 cup	sugar	250 mL
1 cup	water	250 mL
1 cup	orange juice concentrate	250 mL
3 tbsp.	Grand Marnier	45 mL

Cake*:

¾ cup	butter OR margarine	175 mL
2 cups	white sugar	500 mL
2	eggs	2
1 tsp.	vanilla	5 mL
3 cups	flour	750 mL
2 tsp.	baking soda	10 mL
½ tsp.	salt	2 mL
2 cups	buttermilk OR sour milk**	500 mL

1. The night before making the cake, carefully slice the outer peel from an orange, being careful not to include any of the white. Cut the peel into thin slivers. Soak the peel in the sugar and water and let it stand overnight. This reduces the bitterness in the peel.
2. To make the cake, cream the butter and sugar. Add the eggs and vanilla and beat well.
3. Combine the flour, baking soda and salt. Add to the creamed mixture alternately with buttermilk, making 3 dry and 2 liquid additions. After each addition, mix until just blended.
4. Pour batter into a greased 10" (25 cm) bundt pan. Bake at 350°F (180°C) for 40 minutes, or until done. Remove the cake from the oven, cool 10 minutes, then turn the cake out onto a serving tray.
5. In a small saucepan, combine the orange peel and liquid with the remaining syrup ingredients. Simmer for 5 minutes.
6. Pour half the hot syrup over the hot cake. Spoon the remainder of the sauce over the cake slices as it is served. This can be served right away, or chilled. It keeps well overnight.

Serves 16.

SERVING SUGGESTION: Serve hot or cold, with whipped cream and a slice of fresh orange.

* *If you are really in a hurry, a yellow cake mix may be substituted for the scratch cake.*
** *For sour milk, put 2 tbsp. (30 mL) lemon juice or vinegar in a measuring cup and fill it with milk to 2 cups (500 mL).*

White Chocolate-Filled Banana Cake

Start early in the day for this delicacy. Filling and cake need time to cool before assembling, as does the chocolate drizzled on for the finishing touch.

White Chocolate Filling:

3 cups	whipping cream (divided)	750 mL
8 oz.	pkg. white chocolate chips	225 g

Banana Cake:

¾ cup	shortening	175 mL
1½ cups	white sugar	375 mL
2	eggs	2
1 cup	mashed bananas	250 mL
2 cups	flour	500 mL
1 tsp.	EACH baking soda and baking powder	5 mL
½ tsp.	salt	2 mL
½ cup	buttermilk OR sour milk	125 mL
1 tsp.	vanilla	5 mL
½ cup	chopped pecans (optional)	125 mL
1 or 2	bananas, sliced	1 or 2
½ cup	semisweet chocolate (3 oz. [90 g])	125 mL
½ cup	whipping cream	125 mL

1. FILLING: Heat **1½ cups (375 mL)** whipping cream to boiling. Pour over white chocolate in a large bowl. Whisk until chocolate is melted and mixture is smooth. Refrigerate for 5 hours. Then whip remaining 1½ cups (375 mL) cream with electric mixer until stiff but not dry. Whip the white chocolate mixture at medium speed until it is as thick as the whipped cream. Fold the whipped cream into the chocolate mixture.

2. CAKE: With an electric mixer, cream together the shortening and sugar until light and fluffy. Add eggs and beat for 2 minutes. Add bananas and beat for 2 minutes more.

3. Combine flour, baking soda, baking powder and salt. Add dry ingredients alternately with buttermilk to creamed mixture, beating well after each addition. Add vanilla; beat 2 minutes. Stir in pecans.

4. Turn into 2 greased and floured 9" (23 cm) round cake pans. Bake at 375°F (190°C) for 25-30 minutes, or until a toothpick inserted in center of cake comes out clean. Cool in pans on racks for 10 minutes. Remove cakes from pans and cool on racks.

5. Cut cakes into 2 layers. Spread filling between the 4 layers and on top, but not down sides of cake. Place banana slices in middle layer and on top layer.

9. In the microwave on medium, or on stove over low heat, melt together the chocolate and cream. Let cool. Pour chocolate mixture over banana slices, let it drip down the sides of the cake.

Final Temptations

Gingerbread Cake & Lemon Sauce

An old standby that will surely elicit the exclamation – "Oh, I haven't had that for a long time!" The lemon sauce makes this one really special.

Gingerbread Cake:

½ cup	molasses	125 mL
1	egg	1
¼ cup	white sugar	60 mL
1½ cups	flour	375 mL
1½ tsp.	baking soda	7 mL
½ tsp.	salt	2 mL
½ tsp.	EACH cinnamon, nutmeg, ginger	2 mL
¼ tsp.	cloves	1 mL
¼ cup	vegetable oil	60 mL
½ cup	hot water	125 mL

Lemon Sauce:

3 tbsp.	cornstarch	45 mL
¾ cup	white sugar	175 mL
¼ tsp.	salt	1 mL
¾ cup	boiling water	175 mL
2	egg yolks, beaten	2
1 tbsp.	butter OR margarine	15 mL
1 tsp.	fresh grated lemon peel OR ½ tsp. (2 mL) dried	5 mL
¼ cup	lemon juice	60 mL

1. To make the cake, in a large bowl with an electric mixer, thoroughly mix molasses, egg and sugar.
2. Add flour, baking soda, salt and spices. Beat well. The mixture will be quite thick. Add oil and hot water and beat well.
3. Pour the batter into a greased 8" (20 cm) square pan. Bake at 350°F (180°C) for 30-35 minutes, or until a toothpick inserted in the middle of the cake comes out clean. Cool the cake in the pan on a rack OR serve it warm from the pan.
4. For sauce, combine cornstarch, sugar and salt in a heavy saucepan. Gradually add boiling water. Cook, stirring, until thick and clear.
5. Carefully stir ½ cup (125 mL) of the hot mixture into the beaten egg yolks. Return this egg mixture to the saucepan and, stirring constantly, cook over low heat for 2-3 minutes.
6. Remove from heat and stir in the butter, lemon peel and juice. Serve warm or cool over the gingerbread.

Serves 9. Double recipe for a 9 x 13" (23 x 33 cm) pan.

See photograph on page 191.

Miami Beach Birthday Cake

Helen has been serving this light chocolate cake for birthdays for years.

1 cup	semisweet chocolate chips	250 mL
½ cup	graham cracker crumbs	125 mL
⅓ cup	butter OR margarine, melted	75 mL
½ cup	chopped walnuts OR pecans	125 mL
½ cup	butter OR margarine	125 mL
1½ cups	white sugar	375 mL
2	eggs	2
1 tsp.	vanilla	5 mL
2 cups	flour	500 mL
1 tsp.	baking soda	5 mL
1 tsp.	salt	5 mL
1¼ cups	buttermilk OR sour milk*	300 mL
1 cup	whipping cream	250 mL
2 tbsp.	white sugar	30 mL

1. Preheat oven to 375°F (190°C). Grease 2, 9" (23 cm) round cake pans.
2. Melt ⅓ cup (75 mL) chocolate chips on medium heat in microwave about 2 minutes or low heat on stovetop.
3. Combine graham crumbs and melted butter. Stir in walnuts and ⅔ cup (150 mL) chocolate chips. Set aside.
4. In a large mixing bowl, cream butter and 1½ cups (375 mL) sugar and mix until light and fluffy. Add eggs and beat well. Blend in melted chocolate and vanilla.
5. In a separate bowl, mix flour, baking soda and salt. Add to creamed mixture alternately with buttermilk, mixing well after each addition.
6. Pour into prepared pans. Sprinkle with crumb mixture. Bake for 30-40 minutes, or until a toothpick inserted in center of cakes comes out clean. Cool cakes in the pan for 10 minutes, then turn out onto racks to cool, crumb side up. Frost when cooled.
7. Beat cream with 2 tbsp. (30 mL) sugar until stiff. Frost tops of both cakes with whipped cream. Keeping layers top-side up, place one layer on top of the other. Sides are bare. Refrigerate until ready to serve.

Serves 12-16.

* *To make sour milk, put 4 tsp. (20 mL) lemon juice in a measuring cup. Add enough milk to make 1¼ cups (300 mL).*

Desserts – Wild Berries

White Chocolate Cranberry Cake, page 168
Wild Berry Cobbler, page 179

Raspberry Walnut Torte

It may not look spectacular but it tastes soooo good!

1 cup	flour	250 mL
⅓ cup	icing sugar	75 mL
½ cup	butter OR margarine, softened	125 mL
10 oz.	pkg. frozen raspberries, thawed	283 g
¾ cup	chopped walnuts	175 mL
2	eggs	2
1 cup	white sugar	250 mL
½ tsp.	salt	2 mL
¼ cup	flour	60 mL
½ tsp.	baking powder	2 mL
1 tsp.	vanilla	5 mL
	whipped cream OR ice cream for garnish	

Raspberry Sauce:

½ cup	cold water	125 mL
½ cup	white sugar	125 mL
2 tsp.	cornstarch	10 mL
½ cup	reserved raspberry juice (approx.)	125 mL
1 tbsp.	lemon juice	15 mL

1. Combine 1 cup (250 mL) flour, icing sugar and butter and blend well. Press mixture into bottom of a 9 x 13" (23 x 33 cm) pan. Bake at 350°F (180°C) for 15 minutes.
2. Drain the raspberries, reserving liquid for sauce. Spoon the raspberries over the crust and sprinkle with walnuts.
3. In a small mixing bowl, beat the eggs with the sugar until light and fluffy. Add salt, ¼ cup (60 mL) flour, baking powder and vanilla. Blend well and pour over walnuts.
4. Bake at 350°F (180°C) for 30-35 minutes, or until golden brown. Cool in the pan.
5. Combine all the sauce ingredients, except lemon juice, in a saucepan. Cook, stirring constantly, until thickened and clear. Remove the saucepan from the heat, stir in lemon juice and let cool.
6. Cut the torte into squares and serve with whipped cream or ice cream and Raspberry Sauce.

Serves 12.

Marie with Canada Geese at Dymond Lake.

Crazy Cake

Your kids will love this moist, rich chocolate cake, with a choice of 2 toppings.

Chocolate Cake:

3 cups	flour	750 mL
2 cups	sugar	500 mL
½ cup	cocoa	125 mL
2 tsp.	baking soda	10 mL
1 tsp.	salt	5 mL
1 tsp.	vanilla	5 mL
¾ cup	oil	175 mL
2 tbsp.	vinegar	30 mL
2 cups	water	500 mL

Crunchy Buttercream Icing:

¼ cup	butter OR margarine	60 mL
1 cup	icing sugar	250 mL
2	egg yolks	2
1 cup	nondairy whipped topping	250 mL
2	Skor (or Heath) candy bars, frozen and crushed	2

1. CAKE: Combine the dry ingredients in a large bowl. Make a well in the center and add liquid ingredients. Mix well with an electric mixer.
2. Pour batter into a greased 9 x 13" (23 x 33 cm) cake pan. Bake at 350°F (180°C) for 40 minutes, or until done. Let cool.
3. ICING: Cream the butter, icing sugar and egg yolks. Fold in the whipped topping and candy bars.
4. Spread the icing on the cooled cake and refrigerate for a few hours.

Serves 12-16.

OR   Praline Topping: (spread over hot cake)

¼ cup	butter OR margarine	60 mL
6 tbsp.	evaporated milk	90 mL
⅔ cup	brown sugar	150 mL
⅔ cup	shredded unsweetened coconut	150 mL
⅓ cup	chopped pecans OR walnuts	75 mL

1. While the cake is baking, mix all the topping ingredients together and blend well. Spread on the hot cake and place under the broiler until the topping is bubbly and slightly browned, 2-3 minutes. Watch carefully.

Cinnamon Pecan Apple Cake

This is one cake where the edge pieces disappear first – they soak up the most caramel sauce!

1 cup	vegetable oil	250 mL
2 cups	white sugar	500 mL
3	eggs	3
1¼ tsp.	vanilla	7 mL
2 cups	flour	500 mL
1 tsp.	salt	5 mL
1 tsp.	cinnamon	5 mL
1 tsp.	baking soda	5 mL
3 cups	pared, diced apples	750 mL
1 cup	chopped pecans OR walnuts	250 mL

Caramel Topping:

½ cup	butter OR margarine	125 mL
1 cup	brown sugar	250 mL
¼ cup	milk	60 mL

1. To make the cake, beat together oil, sugar, eggs and vanilla. Beat 3 minutes at medium speed if you are using a mixer, slightly longer if you are beating by hand.
2. Mix the flour, salt, cinnamon and baking soda and add to the sugar mixture. Mix well. Stir in the apples and nuts.
3. Spread the batter in a greased 9 x 13" (23 x 33 cm) pan and bake at 350°F (180°C) for 1 hour.
4. When the cake is almost finished baking, prepare the Caramel Topping. In a heavy saucepan combine the topping ingredients and boil for 3 minutes.
5. Pour the topping over the hot cake. Let the cake sit for a couple of hours before serving.

Serves 15.

Caramel Apple Crisp

The addition of baking soda to the apples gives the unmistakable flavor of candy apples. A guaranteed people pleaser!

½ cup	butter OR margarine	125 mL
1 cup	packed brown sugar	250 mL
¼ cup	corn syrup	60 mL
½ tsp.	salt	2 mL
½ tsp.	vanilla	2 mL
¼ tsp.	baking soda	1 mL
8 cups	peeled, sliced tart apples*	2 L
2 tbsp.	flour	30 mL

Crumb Topping:

2 tbsp.	flour	30 mL
2 tbsp.	white sugar	30 mL
1 tsp.	cinnamon	5 mL
1 tbsp.	butter OR margarine	15 mL

1. In a large saucepan, combine the butter, sugar, corn syrup and salt. Bring to a full rolling boil and boil for 5 minutes. Add the vanilla and baking soda.
2. Coat the apples with the flour. Add to the sauce in saucepan. The sauce will form clumps of caramel when the cold apples are added. Cook and stir until clumps melt and mixture is slightly thickened.
3. Pour into a greased, 8-9" (20-23 cm) square pan.
4. Mix flour, sugar and cinnamon. Cut in the butter until crumbly. Sprinkle over the apple mixture.
5. Bake at 400°F (200°C) for 1 hour, or until apples are soft. Put foil or pan under dish to catch the drips.

Single recipe serves 6. Double recipe for a 9 x 13" (23 x 33 cm) pan.

SERVING SUGGESTION: *Serve in a bowl, hot or cold with whipped cream or ice cream.*

* *If using frozen apples, sightly thaw apples first, include all the juice and increase flour to 4 tbsp.(60 mL), to be mixed in with apples.*

Wild Berry Cobbler

A biscuit, rather than a cake, this dessert lends itself to whatever berries you have access to. We like this mixture of berries native to northern Manitoba.

2 cups	blueberries	500 mL
2 cups	cranberries	500 mL
4 cups	crowberries*	1 L
3 tbsp.	lemon juice	45 mL
1½ cups	sugar	375 mL
½ cup	flour	125 mL
1 tsp.	salt	5 mL
3 tbsp.	butter OR margarine	45 mL

Biscuit Dough:

2 cups	flour	500 mL
4 tsp.	baking powder	20 mL
2 tbsp.	white sugar	30 mL
1 tsp.	salt	5 mL
½ cup	shortening OR butter OR margarine	125 mL
⅔ cup	milk	150 mL
1	egg	1

1. Combine mixed berries and lemon juice. In a separate bowl, combine sugar, flour and salt, and pour over the berries. Mix thoroughly and pour into a greased 9 x 13" (23 x 33 cm) baking pan. Dot with butter. Bake in a preheated 400°F (200°C) oven for 15 minutes, or until the berries are hot and bubbling.
2. While the berries are baking, prepare the biscuit dough. Mix together the flour, baking powder, sugar and salt. With a pastry blender, cut in the shortening until the mixture resembles coarse meal. Beat together milk and egg and add to the flour mixture. Stir with a fork until just blended.
3. Remove hot berry mixture from oven. Drop biscuit dough by the spoonful onto the hot berries, distributing evenly over the pan. Return to hot oven and bake about 20 minutes.

Serves 12-15.

SERVING SUGGESTION: Invert each serving onto a plate, berry side up. Top with whipped cream. Serve hot or cold.

* *The crowberries don't really have a flavor of their own, but absorb the flavor of the other two. Since they are more abundant and easier to pick, they can easily make up half the amount of berries.*

See photograph on page 173.

Rhubarb Crunch

Similar to a rhubarb crisp, but with a crunchy crust, top and bottom.

1 cup	flour	250 mL
¾ cup	quick rolled oats	175 mL
1 cup	firmly packed brown sugar	250 mL
½ cup	melted butter OR margarine	1252 mL
1 tsp.	cinnamon	5 mL
4 cups	diced rhubarb, fresh OR frozen	1 L
1 cup	white sugar	250 mL
2 tbsp.	cornstarch	30 mL
1 cup	water	250 mL
1 tsp.	vanilla	5 mL
	whipped cream	

1. Combine flour, oats, brown sugar, butter and cinnamon in a bowl. Mix until crumbly. Press half of crumbs in a greased 9" (23 cm) cake pan. Cover with rhubarb.
2. Combine white sugar, cornstarch, water and vanilla in a small saucepan. Cook, stirring constantly until thick and clear. Pour over rhubarb. Top with remaining crumbs.
3. Bake at 350°F (180°C) for 1 hour. Cut in squares. Serve warm or cold with a dollop of whipped cream.

Serves 6-9.

VARIATION: Doubles well in a 9 x 13" (23 x 33 cm) pan. Increase time by 10 minutes. Freezes well.

Cranberry Pecan Pie

The slight tang of cranberries combined with the sweetness of pecan pie makes this a very agreeable marriage of flavors.

1	unbaked, 9" (23 cm) pie shell	1
3	eggs, beaten	3
1 cup	golden corn syrup	250 mL
⅔ cup	white sugar	150 mL
¼ cup	butter OR margarine, melted	60 mL
2 cups	fresh OR frozen cranberries	500 mL
1 cup	pecan halves	250 mL
	sweetened whipped cream	

Cranberry Pecan Pie

Continued

1. Prepare pie shell. Preheat oven to 425°F (220°C).
2. Mix eggs with corn syrup and set aside.
3. Combine sugar, melted butter, cranberries and pecans and spoon into unbaked pie shell. Carefully pour syrup mixture over filling.
4. Bake at 425°F (220°C) for 10 minutes, then lower temperature to 350°F (180°C) and continue baking for about 40 minutes. When it is set like gelatin when you gently shake the plate, the pie is done.
5. Cool pie to room temperature before slicing. Serve at room temperature or chilled. Top with whipped cream.

Serves 6-8.

Pumpkin Pie Squares

This recipe replaces two pies and it tastes just as good.

1 cup	flour	250 mL
½ cup	quick-cooking rolled oats	125 mL
½ cup	firmly packed brown sugar	125 mL
½ cup	butter OR margarine, softened	125 mL
2 cups	pumpkin, canned OR cooked	500 mL
13½ oz.	can evaporated milk	385 mL
2	eggs	2
¾ cup	white sugar	175 mL
½ tsp.	salt	2 mL
1 tsp.	cinnamon	5 mL
½ tsp.	ginger	2 mL
¼ tsp.	cloves	1 mL
½ cup	chopped pecans	125 mL
½ cup	firmly packed brown sugar	125 mL
2 tbsp.	butter OR margarine	30 mL
	whipped cream	

1. Combine flour, oats, ½ cup (125 mL) brown sugar and ½ cup (125 mL) butter. Mix until crumbly. Press into an ungreased 9 x 13" (23 x 33 cm) pan. Bake at 350°F (180°C) for 15 minutes.
2. Combine pumpkin, evaporated milk, eggs, sugar, salt and spices in a bowl and blend well. Pour over baked crust. Bake at 350°F (180°C) for 20 minutes.
3. Combine pecans, ½ cup (125 mL) brown sugar and 2 tbsp. (30 mL) butter. Sprinkle over pumpkin. Return to oven and bake 15-20 minutes more, or until filling is set. Cool in pan on a rack. Serve chilled or at room temperature, with a dollop of whipped cream.

Serves 12.

Rice Pudding Suprême

This is quite simply the best rice pudding I have ever tasted. It is sooooo creamy! Helen and I were both treated to this pudding by her sister-in-law, Merelyn, and it has become a favorite.

6 cups	whole milk	1.5 L
¾ cup	long-grain rice (not instant)	175 mL
1 cup	cereal cream OR evaporated milk	250 mL
¾ cup	white sugar	175 mL
3	egg yolks, beaten	3
2 tsp.	vanilla extract	10 mL
¼ tsp.	salt	1 mL
½-1 tsp.	cinnamon	2-5 mL
	raisins (optional)	

1. Rinse medium saucepan with cold water. Do not dry. Pour in the milk and bring to a boil over medium heat. Stir in rice and return to a boil over medium heat. Reduce heat and simmer, uncovered, until rice is tender, stirring occasionally, about 30 minutes.
2. In a small bowl, combine cream, sugar, egg yolks, vanilla and salt. When rice is tender, stir the cream mixture into the rice. Heat to boiling point, stirring constantly.
3. Remove pudding from heat, pour into a serving dish. Raisins can be added at this point, if you like. Sprinkle with cinnamon and chill for 2 hours before serving.

Makes 8 cups (2 L).

SERVING SUGGESTION: For a distinctly Canadian treat serve with a spoonful of maple syrup drizzled over each serving.

Mr. Payne and Mr. Stephens were lunching together. As their various friends passed the table, Mr. Payne would stop them and, in glowing terms, describe his success on his recent fishing trip. Stephens, amused by the enthusiastic Mr. Payne, finally said, "Say, I notice that in telling about that fish you changed the size of it for each different listener." "Yes, sure, I never tell a man more than I think he will believe."

Creamy Caramel Flan

"Smooth" is the best word to describe this dessert. It looks like a caramel custard, but is a little richer in flavor. Don't let the caramelized sugar scare you; it is quite easy, but the whole dessert does have to be made a day ahead!

¾ cup	white sugar	175 mL
8 oz.	cream cheese, softened	250 g
5	eggs	5
13½ oz.	can evaporated milk	385 mL
10 oz.	can sweetened condensed milk	300 mL
1 tsp.	vanilla	5 mL

1. In a heavy saucepan, over medium-low heat, cook and stir sugar until melted and golden, about 5 minutes. Quickly pour into an UNGREASED, 2-quart (2 L), round baking or soufflé dish, tilting to coat bottom of pan. Let stand for 10 minutes. NOTE: Do NOT use a pan with a removable bottom.
2. In a mixing bowl, beat the cream cheese until smooth. Add the eggs and beat until thoroughly combined. Add the remaining ingredients and mix well. Pour over the caramelized sugar.
3. Place the 2-quart (2 L) pan in a larger pan (any shape will do) and pour boiling water into the larger pan until it comes about 1" (2.5 cm) up the sides. Bake at 350°F (180°C) for 50-60 minutes, until mixture is just set. (Mixture will jiggle, and a knife, when inserted, will come out clean.)
4. Remove 2-quart (2 L) pan from the larger pan. Set on a wire rack and let cool 1 hour. Refrigerate overnight. To remove flan from pan, run a knife around the edges. Turn over onto a serving dish, preferably with sides, as some of the caramelized sugar will run down the sides of the flan.

Serves 12-16.

SERVING SUGGESTION: Garnish with fresh fruit on the side.

See photograph on page 191.

Brandy Snap Fruit Baskets

A very classy special-occasion dessert that will make you proud! Make it whenever fresh fruit is available.

½ cup	flour	125 mL
½ tsp.	ground ginger	2 mL
6 tbsp.	butter	90 mL
¼ cup	white sugar	60 mL
¼ cup	corn syrup	6 mL
1 tsp.	brandy	5 mL
½	lemon, grated peel of, OR ½ tsp. (2 mL) dried	½

fresh fruit, strawberries, raspberries, blueberries,
   peach slices, etc.
whipped cream

1. Preheat oven to 350°F (180°C). With a nonstick spray, spray 4 round pie or cake pans, 8-9" (20-23 cm) across. Also spray the bottom and outside of 2 upside-down glasses or jars, 2-3" (5-7 cm) across.
2. Sift flour and ginger into small bowl; set aside
3. In a medium saucepan, heat butter, sugar and corn syrup over low heat until butter is melted and sugar is dissolved. It doesn't have to come to a boil. Remove from heat. Add flour mixture and stir until smooth. Stir in brandy and lemon peel.
4. Drop about 2 tbsp. (30 mL) of batter in the center of each pan. Pat the dough down with your fingers to spread it as thinly as possible. It will spread more while baking, so it doesn't have to be spread to the edges of the pans.
5. Bake the cookies, 2 pans at a time, for 10-15 minutes, or until they are uniformly DARK golden brown. Remove only 1 from the oven and proceed quickly with step 6 before removing the second cookie.
6. Allow the cookie to cool on the pan for 15-30 seconds but do not allow it to harden. Remove the cookie with a spatula and drop it over the bottom of the prepared glass or small jar. It will fall down around the sides to form a lacy basket. Mould it around the glass gently but quickly with your hands. If the cookie splits near the base, hold it in place with a towel while it hardens (about 30 seconds). Allow it to harden and remove it from the glass.
7. Remove the second cookie from the oven and repeat step 6.
8. Repeat steps 4-7 until all baskets are made.

Makes 6-8 baskets.

TO SERVE: Fill baskets with fresh fruit in season. Add a dollop of whipped cream and garnish with fresh fruit or mint leaves.

See photograph on page 191.

Chocolate Fondue

A fresh fruit tray makes a superb appetizer before a meal or a grand finale as a dessert. Here is a great chocolate dip to complement the fruit of your choice.

Chocolate Fondue:

12 oz.	Toblerone OR other, good quality	340 g
	semisweet chocolate OR milk chocolate	
¼ cup	whipping cream	60 mL
1 tbsp. +	amaretto, Kahlúa, Tia Maria OR Grand Marnier	15 mL +
	fruit slices of your choice, strawberries, bananas,	
	oranges, peaches, pears, fresh or dried apricots	

1. Melt the chocolate in a double boiler or over very low heat. Stir constantly. When melted, add cream and liqueur; stir to keep smooth.
2. Pour chocolate into a serving dish and surround with fruit. You may use a fondue pot to keep it warm but, unless it has to sit for a long time, it isn't essential.

Makes 1¾ cups (425 mL).

Tia Maria Torte

Shari's unbaked dessert – so simple and so rewarding. Great with Chewy Chocolate Chip Cookies, page 92, but very acceptable with the store-bought variety.

3 cups	whipping cream	750 mL
½ cup	white sugar	125 mL
2 tbsp.	Tia Maria*	30 mL
40	chocolate chip cookies	40
	more Tia Maria	
	shaved chocolate	

1. Whip the cream with sugar and Tia Maria, until very stiff. (Be careful you don't turn it to butter!)
2. In a 10" (25 cm) springform pan, place a layer of cookies. Brush with Tia Maria. Spread a layer of whipped cream over top. Repeat until all the cookies and cream are used up, ending with a layer of cream. Cover with shaved chocolate.
3. Refrigerate until well chilled – at least 2 hours.

Serves 12-16.

* *Try Kahlúa, amaretto or Grand Marnier if you prefer.*

Chocoholic Cheesecake

Chocolate crust, double chocolate filling, chocolate glaze – and for a REALLY superb taste treat, raspberry liqueur!

Chocolate Crumb Crust:

1 cup	crushed chocolate wafers	250 mL
3 tbsp.	butter OR margarine, melted	45 mL

Chocolate Raspberry Filling:

3 x 8 oz.	cream cheese, softened	3 x 250 g
¾ cup	white sugar	175 mL
3	large eggs	3
1 tsp.	vanilla	5 mL
3 x 1 oz.	squares white chocolate, melted	3 x 30 g
¼ cup	raspberry schnapps OR framboise liqueur OR wine (optional)*	60 mL
3 x 1 oz.	squares semisweet chocolate, melted	3 x 30 g

Chocolate Cream Glaze:

6 tbsp.	whipping cream	90 mL
3 x 1 oz.	squares semisweet chocolate, chopped	3 x 30 g

1. To make the crust, combine crumbs and butter. Press mixture onto the bottom of a 9" (23 cm) springform pan. Bake at 350°F (180°C) for 10 minutes.
2. To make the filling, blend cream cheese and sugar with an electric mixer. Add eggs, 1 at a time, mixing well after each addition. Add vanilla.
3. Remove ½ of the batter to another bowl. Stir melted white chocolate and liqueur into this portion. To remaining batter, blend in melted semi-sweet chocolate.
4. Pour the brown chocolate batter over the baked crust and spread evenly. Spoon the white batter carefully over top and spread evenly.
5. Bake at 425°F (220°C) for 10 minutes. Reduce heat to 250°F (120°C) and bake for 30-35 minutes longer, or until center of cake is just barely firm. Remove from oven and immediately run knife around sides. Let cheesecake cool completely before removing the sides of the pan.
6. To make the glaze, in a small, heavy saucepan, bring the cream to a simmer over low heat. Add the chocolate and stir until melted and smooth. Spoon the glaze over the cake. With a metal spatula, spread glaze to cover the top, allowing some to run over the sides.

Serves 10-12.

  Final Temptations

Orange Chocolate Swirl Cheesecake

A slightly more complicated, baked cheesecake. Save this for a day when you have time to fuss. Enjoy the wonderful combination of orange with chocolate.

Orange Graham Crust:

1½ cups	graham wafer crumbs	375 mL
¼ cup	white sugar	60 mL
⅓ cup	butter OR margarine, melted	75 mL
1 tbsp.	grated fresh orange rind OR 1½ tsp. (7 mL) dried	15 mL

Orange Chocolate Filling:

4 x 1 oz.	squares semisweet chocolate	4 x 30 g
3 x 8 oz.	cream cheese	3 x 250 g
1 cup	white sugar	250 mL
5	eggs, room temperature*	5
2 tbsp.	orange liqueur	30 mL
1 tsp.	grated fresh orange rind OR ½ tsp. (2 mL) dried	5 mL

1. Preheat oven to 350°F (180°C).
2. Combine ingredients for crust. Press into the bottom and 1" (2.5 cm) up the sides of a 9" (23 cm) springform pan. Set aside.
3. Melt chocolate on medium in microwave, about 3 minutes, or over low heat on stovetop. Set aside to cool slightly.
4. Using an electric mixer, beat cream cheese with sugar until smooth. Add eggs, 1 at a time, beating just until blended. Beat in liqueur and orange rind.
5. Remove 2 cups (500 mL) of the cheese mixture to a separate bowl. Fold in the melted chocolate and stir by hand until well blended.
6. Pour remaining cheese mixture into prepared pan. Add spoonfuls of the chocolate cheese mixture and carefully zig-zag a spatula or knife through the batter to create a marbled effect.
7. Wrap a large piece of heavy foil around the bottom and sides of the springform pan, then set the pan in a larger pan. Pour water in the larger pan, to come at least 1" (2.5 cm) up the sides of the springform pan. (The foil is to prevent any water from getting at the cheesecake.)
8. Bake at 350°F (180°C) for 35-40 minutes, or until cheesecake is set. Remove cake from oven. Remove pan from foil and place on a cooling rack. IMMEDIATELY run a knife around the rim of the pan to loosen the cake and prevent cracking. Cool thoroughly at room temperature. Chill before serving.

Serves 12-16.

* *To bring cold eggs to room temperature, place them in hot (not boiling) water for a couple of minutes.*

Cranberry Orange Cheesecake

Orange-flavored cheesecake with a tart, cranberry topping – and, by carefully choosing low-fat ingredients, you can make this cheesecake into a healthy choice, without sacrificing good taste! (Margarine, cottage cheese, cream cheese and yogurt all have low-fat options.)

Graham Crust:

1 cup	graham crumbs	250 mL
1 tbsp.	butter OR margarine	15 mL

Filling:

2 cups	cottage cheese	500 mL
8 oz.	cream cheese, softened	250 g
⅔ cup	white sugar	150 mL
½ cup	plain yogurt	125 mL
¼ cup	flour	60 mL
2	egg whites	2
1	egg	1
1 tbsp.	grated orange rind	15 mL
1 tsp.	vanilla	5 mL

Cranberry Orange Topping:

2 cups	cranberries, fresh OR frozen	500 mL
½ cup	orange juice	125 mL
½ cup	white sugar	125 mL

1. Combine crust ingredients. Press over bottom of 9" (23 cm) spring-form pan. Bake at 350°F (180 C) for 5 minutes.
2. To make filling, in a food processor or blender, blend cottage cheese until smooth. Add cream cheese and process until smooth. Add remaining filling ingredients and process until smooth.
3. Pour filling onto crust. Bake at 325°F (160°C) for 50-60 minutes, or until almost set in center. Remove from oven and immediately run knife around edge of cake to loosen from rim. Cool on a rack. Chill before serving.
4. For topping, combine cranberries, orange juice and sugar in a saucepan. Bring to a boil, stirring constantly. Simmer for 5 minutes. (Cranberries will start to pop and sauce will start to thicken.) Chill topping, and spread over cake just before serving.

Serves 12.

  *Final Temptations*

Amaretto Mousse Cheesecake

An excellent, unbaked cheesecake. You must make it ahead and allow it to chill for at least 8 hours.

2 cups	graham cracker OR chocolate OR vanilla wafer crumbs	500 mL
½ cup	butter OR margarine, melted	125 mL
1 tbsp.	unflavored gelatin (7 g env.)	15 mL
½ cup	cold water	125 mL
3 x 8 oz.	cream cheese, softened	3 x 250 g
1¼ cups	white sugar	300 mL
5 oz.	evaporated milk	145 mL
1 tsp.	lemon juice	5 mL
⅓ cup	amaretto liqueur*	75 mL
1 tsp.	vanilla extract	5 mL
¾ cup	whipping cream, whipped	175 mL

1. Combine crumbs and butter and press on bottom and 1½" (4 cm) up the sides of a 9" (23 cm) springform pan. Chill.
2. In a small saucepan, sprinkle gelatin over cold water. Let sit 1 minute. Stir over low heat until completely dissolved, about 3 minutes. Set aside.
3. In a large bowl, with an electric mixer, beat cream cheese with sugar until fluffy. Gradually add evaporated milk and lemon juice. Beat for 2 minutes.
4. Gradually beat in gelatin, amaretto and vanilla until thoroughly blended. Fold in whipped cream.
5. Pour into crust. Cover and chill 8 hours or overnight.

SERVING SUGGESTION: Garnish with chocolate curls or chocolate sauce with fresh berries on the side.

Serves 12.

* *If you prefer to omit the amaretto liqueur, increase the cold water to ¾ cup (175 mL) and add ½ tsp. (2 mL) almond extract with the vanilla in step 4.*

A Scottish Grace

O Lord, wha blessed the loaves and fishes,
Look doon upon these twa bit dishes.
And tho' the tatties be but sma',
Lord, mak' them plenty for us a'.
But if our somachs they do fill,
Twill be another miracle.

Frozen Blueberry Swirl Cheesecake

A very good make-ahead dessert for a hot summer day.

Almond Graham Crust:

1 cup	graham wafer crumbs	250 mL
¼ cup	white sugar	60 mL
¼ cup	ground almonds	60 mL
⅓ cup	butter OR margarine, melted	75 mL

Blueberry Filling:

2 cups	blueberries, fresh OR frozen	500 mL
½ cup	white sugar	125 mL
¾ cup	water	175 mL
2 tbsp.	cornstarch	30 mL
2 x 8 oz.	cream cheese, softened	2 x 250 g
4 cups	vanilla ice cream	1 L

1. Combine crust ingredients. Press firmly onto bottom of a well-greased 10" (25 cm) springform pan.
2. Combine blueberries and sugar in a saucepan. Bring to a boil and simmer for 5 minutes.
3. Combine water and cornstarch until smooth and add to the blueberries. Cook until thick and clear. Chill.
2. Using an electric mixer, beat cream cheese until light and fluffy. Gradually add ice cream by spoonfuls and mix until well blended.
3. Spoon cream cheese and cooked blueberries alternately onto crust. Swirl with a knife for a marble effect. Freeze until ready to serve.

Serves 12-16.

SERVING SUGGESTION: Release springform pan and let stand for 15-20 minutes at room temperature to allow ice cream to soften slightly before serving.

Desserts

Brandy Snap Fruit Baskets, page 184
Gingerbread Cake & Lemon Sauce, page 171
Creamy Caramel Flan, page 183

Drumstick Cake

This tastes just like an ice cream drumstick – but don't take my word for it!

1½ cups	graham wafer crumbs	375 mL
½ cup	chopped peanuts	125 mL
¼ cup	melted butter	60 mL
8 oz.	cream cheese	250 g
½ cup	white sugar	125 mL
½ cup	peanut butter	125 mL
2 tbsp.	vanilla	30 mL
4	eggs	4
1 cup	whipping cream, whipped	250 mL
	chocolate syrup	
	chopped peanuts	

1. Mix graham crumbs, chopped peanuts and melted butter. Press into a 9 x 13" (23 x 33 cm) pan.
2. Mix the cream cheese, sugar, peanut butter, vanilla and eggs. Beat until smooth. Fold in the whipped cream. Pour over crust.
3. Spread chocolate syrup over cheese mixture. Sprinkle chopped peanuts over all.
4. Freeze until ready to serve.

Serves 15.

A Fisherman's Toast

Here's to our fisherman brave,
Here's to the fish he caught,
Here's to the ones that got away,
And here's to the ones he bought!

Marie and Helen at the entrance to Dymond Lake.

Icebound

Every once in awhile, it happens that there is still ice on North Knife Lake when the first guests arrive. Such was the case when we flew in with staff and supplies on June 13, 1984. There was just enough water to land the Beaver and taxi to the dock to unload. We then had to move the plane to the creek so that if the wind shifted it wouldn't become locked in the ice. Things were not looking good; we only had four days to get things ready for the guests. The temperature was barely above freezing and the ice wasn't going anywhere very fast. Where were our guests going to fish? Weather is always unpredictable and often surprising at this time of year, but what a treat when we awoke the next morning to a beautiful, sunny day and a high temperature of about 25°C (77°F). By the time the guests arrived on Friday there was plenty of room to fish at the south end, near the lodge, so fish they did for the next two days. The gorgeous weather continued and the ice at the north end started melting and breaking up nicely. On Monday, when the guides all turned up wearing shorts at breakfast, I mentioned that they should be sure to take warm clothes and rain gear on the lake because the weather could change. They all looked at me as if I had two heads! Clarence, one of our guests who was in his 70s, had fished with us a number of times before. As he was leaving he told me he would be back to have coffee with me about 3 o'clock, so I promised to have fresh cinnamon buns waiting for him.

Well, about 1 o'clock, the wind shifted to the north, the clouds moved in and it started to drizzle. When 3 o'clock came and there was no Clarence I got a little concerned and by 4 o'clock I was very anxious. Clarence wasn't one to be late. The weather was getting worse all the time and I decided that I had to send the plane out to see what was up. There also looked to be some fog to the north, so there was no time to procrastinate.

It turned out that the boats had gone north, through some loose ice, to the hot fishing spots and, when the wind shifted, the ice packed solid and locked them in. The pilot found them, thankfully, in a spot where he was able to put down the airplane and pick up the guests, but there was no room for the guides. Not only that, the guides had to stay with the boats and not one of them had listened to my advice that morning about taking warm clothes and rain gear. The guests arrived back safely but by now it was pouring and the fog had socked right in, so the airplane couldn't go back to get the guides. It was decided that a boat would go and take warm clothes and rain gear to the others and try to help them get home. Off they went, and they didn't have any trouble finding them. The scantily clad guides had a huge bonfire going on the beach to try and keep warm in the 10°C (50°F) temperature. Even with warm clothing the trip home was long and arduous. They had to actually get out and pull the boats over the ice and, of course, every once in a while they would break through. Arriving back at the lodge at 2:30 a.m., they were wet, cold and very hungry but they never went out again without extra clothes and their raingear. Some things you just have to learn for yourself!

Jams, Relishes & Sauces

With cranberries being available all year round, they are becoming a more commonly used fruit. We invite you to use them even more often, on toast, or as a condiment in the form of relish, chutney or ketchup. And don't miss the other favorites we've included here – chili sauce and pancake syrup are a must.

Apple Butter

Some say that apple butter came to Canada with the arrival of German settlers and some attribute it to the English. Whether you eat it in German or in English, you're sure to enjoy this traditional, spicy spread.

8 cups	quartered apples*	2 L
4 cups	apple juice OR cider	1 L
1¾ cups	white sugar	425 mL
1 tsp.	ground allspice	5 mL
1 tsp.	cinnamon	5 mL
½ tsp.	ground cloves	2 mL

1. Wash and quarter sufficient apples to give 8 cups (2 L). Do not peel or core them, but you may wish to remove the flower end.
2. In a large saucepan, combine the apples with apple juice. Bring to a boil and simmer until very soft.
3. Press apples through a sieve or strainer to obtain purée.
4. In a large saucepan, combine purée with sugar and spices. Cook over medium heat, stirring frequently until mixture is clear and slightly thickened.
5. Spoon into hot, sterilized jars, see below, and seal.

Makes 2 pints (1 L).

* *If you have made Crab Apple Jelly, page 202 of "Blueberries & Polar Bears", you may use the remaining purée in this recipe to make Crab apple Butter. Use 3 cups (750 mL) of the purée, and follow directions from step 4 of Apple Butter.*

Sterilizing Jars

The best jars to use, of course, are those specially made for preserves. You can purchase replacement inserts for the lids, and so guarantee a good seal no matter how many times you use the jars. We also use any glass jar that comes with a lid that has a rubber seal on the interior. Avoid lids that have cardboard inserts.

I have to confess that we aren't very careful in this area. We usually settle for pouring boiling water over the jars. This is okay if the preserve is going to be eaten fairly quickly, or if it is going to be stored in a refrigerator.

The following two methods are recommended if you don't have an actual sterilizer.

1. Boil the jars in water for 15 minutes and then leave them in the water until needed. Lids need only be boiled for 5 minutes.
2. Heat the jars in a 225°F (110°C) oven for 10 minutes, then turn off the oven and leave the jars there until needed.

  Jams, Relishes & Sauces

Cranapple Jelly

(MARIE) I have a green apple tree in my yard that yields small, tart apples. My freezer always has sliced apples waiting to be used, and I love the apple juice it makes. (I use the recipe for Crab Apple Juice, page 202, "Blueberries & Polar Bears".)

Now, here is a superb jelly with a vibrant red colour. The sauce that is left over after the juice has dripped can then be used in the next recipe, Cranapple Butter. Both are delightful additions to your preserve cellar.

10 cups	prepared tart apples (see below)	2.5 L
4 cups	cranberries	1 L
2 tbsp.	lemon juice	30 mL
	white sugar	

1. Wash apples, and cut them in large chunks (quarters or eighths). Do not peel or core them. (Some people like to remove the stems and flower ends – I've done it both ways.) Place the apples and cranberries in a large pot. The pot should be about ⅔ full. Add water to just cover the fruit. Boil until the skins have split and the pulp is soft, about 15 minutes.
2. Put the pulp and juice in a sieve, and let the juice drip through. You can press on the pulp very gently to help the juice through, but you don't want the pulp to go through yet. When all the juice has drained, press the pulp through the sieve, INTO ANOTHER BOWL. Save this to make Cranapple Butter.
3. Strain the juice through cheesecloth. This will remove any remaining pulp and give a clear jelly. Measure the juice. (There should be about 6 cups [1.5 L]).
4. Put the juice with an equal amount of white sugar into a large, heavy pot, and add the lemon juice. Stir while it comes to a boil, then reduce heat and boil gently for 20-30 minutes. Test jelly occasionally by dropping a drop on a cold surface. It is done when it begins to gel fairly quickly.
5. Pour the jelly into hot, sterilized* jars and seal. Allow to cool.

Makes about 7 cups (1.75 L) of jelly.

* *See note on sterilizing jars on page 196.*

*Lord, may we eat all we are able
Until our stomachs touch the table.*

Cranapple Butter

In the days of the early settler, every part of the apple was preserved in some way. I ought to have been there – I hate to waste anything! This variation on Apple Butter is equally delicious on toast or with meat.

6 cups	cranberry/applesauce pulp*	1.5 L
6 cups	white sugar	1.5 L
⅛ tsp.	salt	0.5 mL
½ tsp.	cinnamon	2 mL
¼ tsp.	ground cloves	1 mL
½	lemon, grated rind and juice of	½

1. *Follow the Cranapple Jelly recipe, page 197, to get the cranberry/applesauce pulp.
2. Place the pulp, sugar, salt and spices in a saucepan.
3. Cook over medium heat, stirring constantly until mixture is clear and slightly thickened.
4. Remove from the heat and add lemon rind and juice.
5. Spoon into hot, sterilized** jars and seal.

Makes about 7 cups (1.75 L).

** *See note on sterilizing jars on page 196.*

Cranberry Chutney

The fruits of a Canadian autumn combined with the zest of citrus will dress up any turkey dinner in fine style.

4 cups	cranberries	1 L
1½ cups	white sugar	375 mL
1 cup	water	250 mL
1 cup	orange juice	250 mL
1 cup	raisins	250 mL
1 cup	chopped walnuts	250 mL
1	apple, peeled and chopped	1
1 tbsp.	orange peel	15 mL
1 tbsp.	lemon peel	15 mL
1 tsp.	ground ginger	5 mL

1. Boil cranberries and sugar in water and orange juice until skins pop, about 10 minutes. Add remaining ingredients. Mix well. Store in refrigerator, in sterilized* jars.

Makes about 8 cups (2 L).

NOTE: This Chutney does not keep very long after opening.

* *See note on sterilizing jars, page 196.*

Cranberry Orange Relish

An uncooked relish that you can serve as a condiment with meat, or with yogurt or ice cream for dessert! It is a great source of Vitamin C!

4 cups	cranberries	1 L
2	oranges	2
1¾ cups	white sugar	425 mL

1. Chop the cranberries coarsely in a food chopper or processor.
2. Cut up oranges and remove seeds. Chop orange pieces, including rind, in food chopper or processor.
3. Mix fruit with sugar and let stand a few hours before serving. Store in the refrigerator. Keeps about 2 weeks. Freezes well for longer periods.

Makes about 4 cups (1 L).

See photograph on page 155.

Cranberry Ketchup

Great on turkey sandwiches, but don't stop there. Try it with hamburgers or grilled fish, a glaze for chicken or ribs, or a dip for grilled cheese.

1 cup	chopped onion	250 mL
2 cups	cranberries	500 mL
½ cup	vinegar	125 mL
2 cups	water	500 mL
1 cup	brown sugar	250 mL
1 tsp.	cinnamon	5 mL
½ tsp.	red pepper flakes	2 mL
1 tsp.	ground ginger	5 mL
½ tsp.	salt	2 mL
	pepper to taste	

1. Cook the onions and cranberries in vinegar and water until onions are soft and cranberries pop. Put in a blender or food processor and purée until smooth.
2. Return the cranberry purée to the saucepan and add remaining ingredients. Cook over medium-low heat, stirring occasionally, for about 20 minutes, or until mixture is thick. Season to taste with more salt or pepper.
3. Ladle ketchup into hot, sterilized* jars and seal.

Makes about 2½ cups (625 mL).

* *See note on sterilizing jars, page 196.*

Chili Sauce

(MARIE) Is there anything as wonderful as the rich aroma of spices brewing in a kettle? I can still smell and taste the chili sauce of my childhood. Why not add these aromas to your kitchen whenever tomatoes are plentiful?

15	ripe medium-sized tomatoes*	15
4	medium onions	4
1	bunch of celery, stalks only**	1
1 cup	vinegar	250 mL
2 tbsp.	salt	30 mL
1 cup	sugar, brown OR white	250 mL
1 tsp.	EACH cinnamon and ground cloves	5 mL

1. Chop tomatoes, onions and celery very fine. Add the remaining ingredients and boil in a large pot for 3-4 hours, or until thick. The volume will be reduced by about one-third.
2. Pour into hot, sterilized*** jars and seal.

Makes 4 quarts (4 L).

* *This recipe is intended as a guide, and the amounts are not written in stone.*
** *Freeze the leaves to use in soup.*
*** *See note on sterilizing jars, page 196.*

Salsa

It is hard to ruin salsa. This recipe is just a guide, and mine never tastes exactly the same twice. The most important determiner of taste is the jalapeños. How hot do you like it? This is a medium salsa, adjust your amounts accordingly.

12-15	ripe tomatoes	12-15
2	large onions	2
1	sweet green pepper	1
¼ cup	jalapeño peppers, fresh OR pickled	60 mL
2	garlic cloves, mashed	2
¼ cup	vinegar	60 mL
1 tsp.	salt	5 mL

1. Chop tomatoes, onions, green pepper and jalapeños. Place them in a large pot and add remaining ingredients. Bring to a boil, reduce heat and simmer for 1-2 hours, until the liquid is reduced.
2. Pour into sterile jars and seal.

Makes approximately 4 quarts (4 L).

Flavored Vinegars

Flavored vinegars add subtle accents to vegetables, salads, sauces & meat dishes.

Herb Vinegar

¾ cup	packed fresh herbs, rosemary, tarragon, basil, thyme, oregano, mint, chives OR dillweed	175 mL
3 cups	white wine vinegar	750 mL

Place the herb in a clean glass bottle; pour vinegar over and seal. Let steep in a dry cool place for 8-10 days. Strain vinegar into a clean bottle and, if you wish, add a decorative sprig of the same herb. Seal bottle.

Makes 3 cups (750 mL).

VARIATIONS: GARLIC VINEGAR: use 9 halved garlic cloves instead of herbs
GINGER VINEGAR: use ¾ cup (175 mL) peeled chopped ginger root instead of herbs.
RASPBERRY VINEGAR: use 3 cups (750 mL) crushed raspberries instead of herbs.

Cranberry Vinegar

3 cups	white wine or cider vinegar	750 mL
1½ cups	cranberries*, fresh OR thawed frozen	375 mL
6 tbsp.	honey	90 mL
	cinnamon sticks and whole cloves	

1. In a saucepan, bring vinegar and half of berries to a boil. Lower heat and simmer 2 minutes. Add honey, stir and strain vinegar into a clean container. Discard cooked berries.
2. In each of 3, 8 oz. (250 mL) bottles, place half of remaining berries, 2 cloves and 1 cinnamon stick. Pour warm vinegar into the bottles and seal. Let steep for 8-10 days.

Makes 3 cups (750 mL).

* *Substitute blueberries to make blueberry vinegar.*

Pancake Syrup

(MARIE) You'll have guests asking what brand you buy! It's a great money saver!

2 cups	brown sugar	500 mL
2½ cups	white sugar	625 mL
½ cup	corn syrup (optional)	125 mL
¼ tsp.	salt	1 mL
2 cups	boiling water	500 mL
½ tsp.	EACH vanilla and maple flavoring or extract	2 mL

1. Mix first 5 ingredients in a saucepan. Bring to a boil and boil for 3 minutes, 5 minutes if not using corn syrup, without stirring. Add flavorings. Let cool. Store in the refrigerator. For longer storage, seal in sterilized jars, see page 196, while hot. Store on a shelf.

Makes 4½ cups (1 L) syrup

Jams, Relishes & Sauces 201

Lime Marmalade

Make this wonderful marmalade any time of the year.

4	limes	4
⅛ tsp.	baking soda	0.5 mL
1¾ oz.	pkg. Certo	50 g
3 cups	water	750 mL
5 cups	sugar	1.25 L
	green food coloring (optional)	

1. Wash limes, cut in quarters lengthwise and scrape out pulp and juice into large saucepan. Discard the white membrane between sections.
2. In a small saucepan, add the baking soda to the lime rinds, cover with water and simmer for 20 minutes. Drain and cool. Scrape or cut all of the white part from the rind. Cut peel lengthwise in very thin slices.
3. Add peel, Certo and 3 cups (750 mL) water to lime pulp in saucepan. Over high heat, bring to a hard boil, stirring occasionally.
4. Add sugar; return to full, rolling boil. Boil hard, stirring, for 1 minute.
5. Remove from the heat and add a few drops of food coloring, if desired. Let set 7 minutes. Skim and discard foam. Pour marmalade into hot, sterilized jars, see page 196, and seal.

Makes approximately 6 cups (1.5 L).

Dried Cranberries

Used as snacks or in baking and sauces, these dried berries are increasingly available in gourmet and grocery stores. Now you can make your own.

½ cup	sugar	125 mL
⅔ cup	water	150 mL
3 cups	fresh cranberries (12 oz. [340 g] bag)	750 mL

1. Combine sugar and water in a small pan. Cook and stir until sugar is dissolved, about 3-4 minutes.
2. Wash cranberries; pat dry. Cut berries in half. Leave wild berries whole.
3. Combine berries and sugar syrup in a bowl. Let stand 2 hours up to overnight. Drain and reserve syrup.
4. Spread berries over lightly greased baking trays. Bake at 175°F (80°C) for 1 hour. Pour reserved syrup over berries and stir to coat well. Bake for another 2 hours, until dried and wrinkled looking, but still slightly soft and flexible. Smaller berries dry more quickly; remove as required.
5. Place berries on a clean surface, do not cover. Let stand in a dry, cool place overnight.
6. Store in airtight container(s). Refrigerate or freeze for up to 2 months.

Index